Evaluating Language

Papers from the
Annual Meeting of the British Association for Applied Linguistics
held at the University of Essex, September 1992

Edited by
David Graddol and Joan Swann

BRITISH ASSOCIATION FOR APPLIED LINGUISTICS

in association with

MULTILINGUAL MATTERS LTD

Clevedon ● Philadelphia ● Adelaide

ISBN 1-85359-238-2 (pbk)

Published by the British Association for Applied Linguistics in association with Multilingual Matters Ltd.

UK: Frankfurt Lodge, Clevedon Hall, Victoria Road, Clevedon, Avon BS21 7SJ.
USA: 1900 Frost Road, Suite 101, Bristol, PA 19007, USA.
Australia: P.O. Box 6025, 83 Gilles Street, Adelaide, SA 5000, Australia.

Typeset by Wayside Books, Clevedon.
Printed and bound in Great Britain by the Longdunn Press, Bristol.

Contents

Preface

The nine papers included in this volume are selected from those presented at the 25th Annual Meeting of the British Association for Applied Linguistics, held at the University of Essex, September 1992.

Each of these papers takes a different approach to the conference theme of 'evaluation'. The first two papers, from invited key-note speakers, take the opportunity that an anniversary offers for reviewing the present state of Applied Linguistics and the relationship between theory and practice which is fundamental to the discipline. But both also address the theme in relation to specific issues: linguists' responses to evaluative and prescriptive interests in language expressed by many non-linguists, and methods of evaluating the competence of children with specific language impairment.

Other papers continue the theme: they consider the evaluation of aspects of the language curriculum, attitudes to language varieties, speaker evaluations as displayed in narratives, inexperienced writers' evaluations of their own texts, language assessment and the language of advertisements. Taken together the collection illustrates something of the breadth and diversity of research which Applied Linguistics in Britain now embraces, and suggests that BAAL can look forward to a further 25 years of rewarding and varied work.

David Graddol and Joan Swann

1 Grammar and Language Impairment: Clinical Linguistics as Applied Linguistics

PAUL FLETCHER
University of Reading

Introduction

The last 10 years or so has seen the burgeoning of a new branch of applied linguistics, often known as *clinical linguistics*. The aim of clinical linguistics is to address the theories, constructs, models and descriptions of modern linguistics, to the speech and language of children and adults diagnosed as language impaired by the professionals — speech and language therapists — who work with them. This work rests on at least two major assumptions. First, it is a general assumption of linguists approaching data from language impairment (taking their lead from Jakobson, 1941; 1968, in relation to phonological breakdown in aphasia) that the deficits identified in affected individuals will not be random with respect to models of linguistic structure. We expect to find the fault lines of an individual's language disorder proceeding along structurally lawful paths, relative to the linguistic frameworks with which we are working. Second, it is assumed that the characterisation of the language impairment that the linguist comes up with will be useful to the speech therapist in two ways. It will provide an assessment of the current state of the impaired individual's language system, relative to some standard of normal performance; and this information will assist in planning remediation. Clinical linguistics, as a young step-sibling of applied linguistics, may not yet be legitimate enough to have its paternity acknowledged. When it is, David Crystal is likely to be most people's choice as the progenitor. It is a quotation of his which we can use to fasten down this initial link between theory and practical matters:

1

remediation presupposes assessment, which presupposes [linguistic] analysis, which presupposes [linguistic] description. (Crystal, 1984: 32)

The terms within square brackets have been supplied to the original, in order to emphasise that the link between linguistics and the patient in the clinic is, on this view, a very direct one, provided the collaboration between linguist and speech therapist is taken into account. That it is possible for a branch of applied linguistics to have such a direct role in cases of inefficient language learning, or language breakdown, will cause at least raised eyebrows among those familiar with a more traditional applied linguistics concerned with the second or foreign language learner. Many of them have become used to a much looser relationship between linguistics, linguists and the practical areas applied linguists are interested in. It is perhaps appropriate on the occasion of the 25th anniversary conference of the British Association for Applied Linguistics to reflect on the character of clinical linguistics, as it moves, roughly speaking, into late adolescence. This transition will inevitably bring change, as the offspring reviews its relationships with its more mature close relatives, and seeks to specify its role in life more precisely. In what follows, I would like to convey something of what clinical linguists do, and indicate some new directions which might improve the linguist-speech therapist collaboration:

(1) First I will use a case of language impairment in an individual child to illustrate the usual approach to the relationship between description, assessment and remediation as outlined in the Crystal quotation above;
(2) I will try to identify some limitations, again in relation to this specific case, of the clinical linguistic approach as practised to date;
(3) I will then use some data from our own research at Reading, in the context of an up-to-date perspective on language learning, to suggest some modifications to the approach.

The case of P.

Any linguist who works in speech and language impairment quickly becomes aware of the two major sources of information about the field: *the case study,* and *the research project.* The research project we will come to later on; however, the bread and butter of the speech and language therapist, and hence of the jobbing clinical linguist, is the case study: speech therapists in general see patients one at a time, for both assessment and remediation, and so this encounter is likely to prove the most common meeting-ground for the speech therapist and the linguist collaborating. This is where we begin our illustration of the role that can be played by clinical linguistics.

The history of one particular case, who we shall refer to as P., is summarised below:

The case of P.

First assessment: 16.10.90 & 23.10.90.

Date of birth: 11.10.82.

C.A. at assessment: 8;0 years.

History: Apart from intermittent hearing infections up to the age of 2;0, no perinatal or later medical history (medical investigation has been thorough, including brain scans and chromosome analysis); hearing now normal.

Language background: Initially raised as French and English speaking, in France; now resident in England and attending a school for children with moderate learning difficulties, and receiving regular speech therapy.

Language history: Very slow development in both languages initially; first word(s) at 2;6; slow development thereafter.

We see then an eight-year-old boy who has shown difficulties with language learning from the start, though not with all language learning. His pronunciation is relatively good. So — not unusually — we find a selective impairment, with one level or module of the grammar (considered most generally) intact, but others not. (Incidentally, the fact that we are seeing a boy is not surprising: about three times as many boys as girls are language-impaired.)

Nor is it surprising that there is no obvious medical history to link to P.'s slow progress. There rarely is. In most cases the only symptom, or the primary symptom, of the problem is the language impairment itself. This has given rise to the widely used term *specific language impairment* (SLI), to refer to inefficient language learning in the absence of any obvious physical cause, and in children whose intellectual capacities are intact, as measured by performance on non-verbal IQ tests. While P.'s language difficulties certainly have no obvious physical cause, it is not clear, in the absence of reliable information on his intellectual status, whether he falls under the SLI heading. Being raised bilingually would certainly have been an added burden for P., and he copes better in a monolingual environment. He has a younger brother, however, who learned both languages successfully. The bilingual background represented an extra hazard for the impaired language learner, rather than constituting any kind of reason for the problem.

The first task of the team investigating an individual's linguistic problems is to provide a summary statement of his current abilities. The information derived from standardised procedures in the initial assessment for P. appears below:

Summary of initial assessment: language age estimates

Receptive:

Reynell Developmental Language Scales (R)	3;0 years.
British Picture Vocabulary Scales	3;0 years.

Expressive:

Mean Length of Utterance	3;0 years.
Renfrew Word-finding Vocabulary Scale	4;2 years.

While for the usual reasons we would not want to interpret these age-estimates too stringently, what they do tell us is that on a number of tests P. is dramatically adrift of his chronological age peers in terms of language ability, and also that the gap is obvious in both comprehension and production. Such standardised procedures do not, however, give us much qualitative information on the nature of P.'s deficit. For this we need to turn to a linguistically more detailed and informed assessment.

Profiling

The initial contribution of clinical linguistics to assessment procedures was the PROFILE: an assessment procedure organised with reference to some part of the linguistic system and designed to summarise, usually in quantitative terms, the performance of an affected individual, where possible relative to some normative data. Profiles have been made available over the last 15 years for a wide range of areas: for phonology, segmental and non-segmental; for dysfluency; for voice; for discourse; for pragmatics even. From this you will gather that speech and language impairments can be recognised in pretty well any area of the language system or its deployment. The area that the group at Reading were most concerned with, however, was a profile of *grammar*.

Linguistic profiling

This profile, as a summary of an individual's syntactic and morphological performance, is usually based on a naturalistic speech sample. Information is listed below from the simplest kind of grammatical profile, namely the distribution of proportions of simple clauses in (on the left-hand side) a sample of 100 utterances from P. On the right-hand side are shown the equivalent data from a group of three-year-old normal children.

P.'s clause structures — first assessment:

	P.	*Normal three-year-olds*
SV	.11	.11
(S)VC(A)	.47	.06
(S)VA(A)	.19	.10
(S)VO(A)	.16	.51
Other	.07	.05

The grammatical description from which the labels used here are derived is the Quirk grammar (Quirk *et al.*, 1985). It will be apparent from the proportions represented in P.'s data that, of the five clause types shown, clauses with direct objects — (S)VO(A) — are under-represented, relative to the proportions of other clause types found in samples of speech from a group of normal three-year-old children. (This group was chosen for comparison because of the convergence, in standardised tests, of estimates of P.'s language age at around three years.) While the Quirk system is not particularly transparent with regard to predicate types, the distinction between O (object) and C (complement) as clause elements allows us to recognise a distinction between clause structures with transitive verbs, and those with copula verbs (e.g. BE, BECOME).

While the normal three-year-old sample show a preponderance of clauses with at least direct objects in their predicate structure, P.'s favourite clause pattern appears to be (S)VC(A). Within the Quirk grammar this sequence is reserved for copula verbs, particularly the verb 'to be', and the C in the sequence is a clause element (complement) following one of these verbs, and realised as NP, PP or AP. The distribution of clause types for P., by comparison with his language age peers, suggested to us at the least, an under-use of lexical verbs, and prompted further investigation in this area. One example of P.'s problems with verbs appears in this extract from the first session in which we saw him:

P.'s verb use: an example

In the course of a word-naming procedure, P. was shown a picture of a saw. This dialogue ensued ('T' = therapist; parentheses indicate repeated elements; — and —— represent pauses of different lengths):

> **T:** what's the next one then
> **P:** a knife
> (cut)——cut the knife
> **T:** what do you cut with that
> 5 **P:** a saw
> have to be careful but it's very sharp

> **T:** you're right
> **P:** daddy — cuts the knife
> **T:** does he cut things with the saw
> 10 **P:** yes
> **T:** what does he cut
> **P:** (cut cut) cut you
> **T:** I don't think so
> **P:** look
> 15 **T:** it won't hurt yourself
> **T:** does he cut food or wood with a saw
> **P:** cuts saw——
> big logs

Here we see him attempting to use the verb CUT, but with difficulty. The first problem he has is in finding the word 'saw'. Subsequently there is ample evidence of the difficulty he has in organising the argument structure — the appropriate postverbal phrasal categories — for the verb CUT.

A digression at this point might be useful to consider what P. as a speaker needs to know about this verb in order to deploy it successfully. Taking the phonological shape for granted, we can identify:

(1) semantic information relating to the action denoted by CUT, and distinguishing from actions which are similar, but different in manner, e.g. HACK, CHOP, or different in their effect on the object, e.g. SEVER, or different in their temporal aspect, e.g. SAW;

(2) knowing that CUT is a verb in English, i.e. that it belongs to the syntactic category VERB;

(3) the action referred to by CUT requires an AGENT; it is an action performed on some object, or THEME; and that the action is performed with some INSTRUMENT;

(4) the AGENT is generally realised syntactically as NP/S[1]; THEME as direct object NP; the INSTRUMENT (when expressed) is realised by a PP. The thematic role and syntactic information (which is where we would argue P.'s problems with the verb are concentrated) for CUT can be summarised thus:

The grammar of CUT
CUT
s(emantic) selection: THEME   INSTRUMENT
c(ategory) selection: +[____   NP   (PP)   ]

If we return briefly to the extract above, we can use this representation to characterise P.'s problems: there are three occasions on which the semantic role of INSTRUMENT (which with this verb requires a PP if it is expressed as an internal argument) is represented by an NP (ll. 3, 8, 17). In the whole sequence, the NP representing the THEME semantic role is omitted; there is only instance where (via a pronominal form) a grammatically appropriate direct object NP appears (l.12). A repair in the final line may represent an attempt at a direct object NP, but the example is equivocal.

We should now consider in summary what information we have about P. on the basis of his assessment.

(1) A number of standardised procedures, for receptive and expressive ability, for lexis and syntax, indicate a considerable discrepancy between P.'s linguistic ability and that of his chronological age peers.

(2) A description and analysis of a spontaneous speech sample reveals a potentially major grammatical deficit in the area of verbs and their argument structures: this knowledge is crucial to the structure of clauses and, while it is not the only grammatical area in which P. shows problems, it is so fundamental as to dictate priority in remediation.

At this point then at least in outline, we have an exemplification of the chain of events decreed in the our original quotation; a description, and an analysis (which, though it is not made explicit in the quote, depends crucially on a comparison with language normal children's performance) produces an assessment. The assessment identifies a priority for remediation, but does not, at least in this case specify or recommend the form or nature of the remediation.

P.'s subsequent history

P. is not a local patient who appears regularly in our clinic. He has, however, been seen twice for review since the initial assessment, and some information from the second of these review sessions appears below:

Third assessement:	9.6.92.
C.A. at assessment:	9;8 years.
Receptive:	
Test for Reception of Grammar:	4;0 years.
(TROG)	
Expressive:	
Renfrew Word-finding Vocabulary Scales	5;1 years.

P.'s clause structures — third assessment:

SV	.23
SVC(A)	.32
SVA	.36
(S)VO(A)	.00
Other	.10

From the standardised procedures, some good news. P. is making slow but measurable progress on standardised tests of comprehension and vocabulary. But the not-so-good news is that he is apparently still failing to manage argument structures as we would expect in his spontaneous speech data, with a continued tendency to avoid verbs with direct objects. A type-token analysis of his lexical verbs finds that he is using more of these now than he was 18 months ago, but he tends to use intransitive verbs with PP adjuncts (see the high proportion of SVA clauses) rather than constructing VPs with internal arguments. Another matter for concern, casting some doubt on his overall awareness of the importance of constituent order to interpret grammatical relations in English, is his inability to deal appropriately in the test of grammar comprehension (TROG) with simple active declarative sentences such as 'the boy is chasing the sheep' and 'the man is chasing the dog'. In both cases he interpreted the animals as doing the chasing, indicating the use of an immature 'probable event strategy' for comprehension (see Chapman, 1978) rather than direct use of constituent order to determine grammatical relations.

Research Groups

So far our discussion relates only to a single case. But how common are verb argument problems in SLI children, and if they do occur, what form do they take? In response to a claim by Myrna Gopnik (Gopnik, 1990b; Gopnik & Crago, 1990) that restricts the effect of SLI on grammar to what are called feature-related (FR) elements such as agreement, tense, number and gender, we have undertaken some work at Reading[2] on a group of SLI children over the last year, which suggests that Gopnik's claim is too restrictive, and that argument structure problems, in particular the omission of obligatory arguments, can be found in a group of SLI children. It is certainly true that the school-age SLI children we looked at, between six and nine years of age, (the age-range into which P. falls) had problems with FR elements. We can identify problems with agreement, with omission of auxiliaries, with past tense, with determiners. The occurrence of these problems is not at issue (see Fletcher, Ingham & Kirby, 1992 for further details).

Our major concern here though is with the occurrence of argument structure problems in relation to lexical verbs. Overall, the errors in verb complementation would not appear to be large-scale: for the language-impaired, 2% of lexical verbs show error, while for the language-normal matches, the figure is 1.45%. Of course the group measure once again conceals individual differences: some of the SLI group make no errors in c-selected elements, while one of them has a 7% error rate. Two points need to be made, however, to put these figures in perspective. First, when we look at feature-related errors, we also find some relatively low proportions.

Second, the lengths of samples over which the rates of omission are computed are relatively small, and this would tend to favour FR elements — generally members of closed grammatical classes — over lexical verbs — which belong to a very large open class — for finding errors. There are simply more obligatory contexts per item. If your control of agreement is shaky, this is likely to reveal itself several times in a sample of 100 clauses. If, by contrast, you do not have full control over the lexical representation for the verb FIND, this may not appear at all in a sample of 100 clauses. If organising the obligatoriness/optionality of NP complements for verbs is a problem for (some) SLI children, this is likely to manifest itself with different verbs with different individuals, resulting in overall low frequencies. Of course this assumption would need to be checked over larger samples. The full details of verb complementation errors appear in Table 1, which are followed by a list of examples:

(a) Overall SLI — Normal comparison

Table 1 Verbs with omitted obligatory complements

A. MATCHED NORMAL GROUP (3 and 5-year-olds)

	OMITTED ELEMENT	
VERB	*NP*	*PP*
put	8	5
bring	1	
got	1	
throw	1	

TOTAL NUMBER ERRORS: 16
TOTAL NUMBER VERBS AFFECTED: 4

B. SLI GROUP (6 years to 9;8 years)

	OMITTED ELEMENT	
VERB	*NP*	*PP*
put	2	6
find	1	
fit		1
get		1
have	1	
let	1	
make	2	
move	1	
take	1	
tell	2	

TOTAL NUMBER ERRORS: 19
TOTAL NUMBER VERBS AFFECTED: 10

(b) Examples of the omission of c-selected elements

(i)   Omission of NP

SLI:

SHE: *put* on there
                    move there

SE: what's that?
E: just this
SE: game to *put* on

DA: you can *take* over there
                    I can take her.

PE: I let them get out.
E: oh dear.
PE: X let out.
PE: don't *let* out

E: really? Have you got a dog?
DA: I *told* already.

DA: there it's something white but I can't *find*.

E: did you look down?
DAM: yeah, (it was it made me) it *made* a little bit scared.

AN: it's got the body, right,
                    and it *tells* how many bones there are.

(ii) Omission of PP

SLI:

ZA: *put* the chair
E: just there.

DA: *put* another chair.

E: somebody's got to sleep in it
DA: I can't *fit* him.

Table 1, and the list of examples following, can be summarised as follows:

(1) The omitted verb argument tends to be NP more often than PP.

(2) There are slightly more errors for the SLI than the LN group, though if we take total sample size into account, this difference is not significant. However, if we exclude the very frequent verb PUT from both halves of the table, there is a clear difference between the two groups.

(3) Whether or not we exclude PUT, the most interesting feature of the tables is the wider range of verbs affected in the LI group. In particular, consider the NP examples under section (b) in the list of examples provided. The examples show three different categories of omission:

— NPs (direct objects) in V-NP-PP structures, e.g. PUT (first example, from Amy);

— NPs in monotransitives;

— PPs (usually location), with verbs that normally c-select for an obligatory NP and PP (usually PUT, but also FIT, for example).

Discussion

The information from our group study confirms that SLI school-age children do have problems with verb argument structure, particularly the provision of obligatory arguments, and indicate that P. is not an isolated case. The question we wish to turn to now is why P., and perhaps other children who are language-impaired, have problems with the learning of verbs and their syntactic complementation. Perhaps we should emphasise that these are persisting problems of complementation. The major distinction to be made between SLI children and normals, on the basis of our data, is that features which are a part of every child's development, but which are effortlessly left behind in the normal acquisition process may 'fossilise' in SLI children's systems. If we compare P. or the SLI group children to their age peers, we find major differences in their grammars: a seven-year-old normal comparison group show virtually no feature-related or argument structure errors. We have to go a long way back down the course of development to find these errors occurring in any frequency in normals. The question then becomes, what is it about the SLI children's language learning mechanism that inhibits or prevents the developmental changes that occur naturally in the normal child?

At this point we need to examine more closely what is involved in the learning of verbs. On a currently influential view of the linguistic representation of verbs; which we have assumed in earlier discussion, there are two levels of a verb's lexical representation. Argument structure, as the lexical level hosting grammatical information, should be distinguished from a verb's lexical semantic level of representation. The latter, referred to a verb's s(emantic) selection, can be couched in terms of the thematic roles relevant to a particular verb. The level at which grammatically relevant information is represented is referred to as c(ategory) selection (for a more extended discussion see Fletcher, Ingham & Kirby, 1992: 115, and the references cited there). The relevance of this view of verb representations for language learning is that a verb's complementation (its c-selection) is not always predictable from its s-selection. In English the omission of subject arguments is ungrammatical, save in certain highly restricted contexts: in informal discourse an utterance-initial subject may be ellipted. Omission of direct objects with English finite verbs is, however, lexically restricted, and is not a regular grammatical process (Ingham, 1992). Consider the pairs below, where verbs with similar meanings, and presumably similar s-selection, differ in the obligatoriness of direct object NP arguments. The first verb in each pair allows omission of the NP, while the second requires the NP to be expressed:

> she won't obey/*respect
> help/*support
> choose/*select

The data suggest that the learning of the c-selection facts of English is not mastered by normal three-year-olds, and occasional problems occur with five-year-olds, but that there are no errors of c-selection with seven-year-olds. In an experimental investigation of the means by which normal children acquire the facts of c-selection (of direct objects), Ingham (1992) reports that normally-developing pre-school children appear to be highly sensitive to syntactic input, in their use and omission of direct objects. As the direct object omission errors of our SLI children continue, it may be the case that they are not as sensitive as normals to syntactic input, and hence less competent at constructing c-selection representations. We would predict that in similar experimental studies the SLI children will show less awareness of syntactic input.

Conclusions

In the early part of this paper we used the profiling approach, a central procedure in clinical linguistics so far, to successfully identify a selective impairment of grammar in a language-impaired child. With the profiling approach we can usefully compare profiles from impaired individuals and matched normals to draw conclusions about the relative distributions of language products, which can certainly be informative. Indeed, such an approach may be a necessary 'first pass' through any data. A study which essentially provided a 'c-selection profile' for lexical verbs, confirmed the existence of direct object omission errors in a group of SLI children of similar age to P. The profiling approach, however, while necessary, was not, to judge from P.'s subsequent history, sufficient to influence successful remediation. To return to the quotation, with which we began this paper, remediation presupposes linguistic assessment, but it also appears to presuppose a great deal more.

Of course many of the decisions that are relevant to remediation are the province of the speech-language therapist and her professional colleagues alone, and nothing to do with linguists. Nevertheless, something appears to have been missing from the speech therapist–linguist collaboration in this case which could be relevant to the linguistic re-education of P. This collaboration requires the assessment information provided by profiling, but also appears to require information about how and under what conditions the missing knowledge about verbs can be acquired. This in turn requires a rather different comparison between normals and SLI children than the profiling approach implies. In addition to quantitative information about clause structures, or even about the errors that normal children make on the way to mastery of the c-selection requirements of verbs, we need to know more about the process of learning them. The next phase of clinical linguistics will benefit from a perspective which considers the learning process in normals in order to discover what is going wrong in non-normal or inefficient learning in SLI children. In this way it could improve the quality of information provided for the speech therapist, strengthen the link between assessment and remediation, and bring theory closer to practical matters.[3]

Notes

1. The situation is in reality more complex than we are representing here: it is possible for CUT to have a subject NP representing the semantic role INSTRUMENT, as in 'this knife wouldn't cut butter'. For the purposes of this discussion we will not pursue this possibility.
2. This work has been carried out with support from the Medical Research Council (grant no. G9015115N), with Gabrielle Kirby and Richard Ingham.
3. I am very grateful to my colleagues Susan Edwards and Richard Ingham, whose comments on an earlier version of this paper led to revisions; they have not had the opportunity to respond to these changes, and so bear no responsibility for the final draft. I would also like to take the opportunity to thank the many speech-language therapists with whom I have worked, in the Department of Linguistic Science at Reading and elsewhere, who have freely given of their time, advice and experience. Without such people clinical linguists could not work.

References

Crystal, D. (1984) *Linguistic Encounters with Language Handicap*. Oxford: Basil Blackwell.

Crystal, D., Fletcher, P. and Garman, M. (1990) *The Grammatical Analysis of Language Disability* (2nd edn). London: Whurr Publishers.

Fletcher, P. (1992) Lexical verbs and language-impairment: A case study. *Clinical Linguistics and Phonetics* 6, 147–54.

Fletcher, P. and Hall, D. (eds) (1992) *Specific Speech and Language Disorders in Children*. London: Whurr Publishers.

Fletcher, P., Ingham, R. and Kirby, G. (1992) The grammatical characterisation of specific language impairment: Theoretical and methodological issues. In R. Ingham and I. Phillipaki-Warburton (eds) *Working Papers in Linguistics*. Department of Linguistic Science, University of Reading.

Gleitman, L. (1990) The structural sources of verb-meaning. *Language Acquisition* 1, 3–55.

Gopnik, M. (1990a) Feature-blind grammar and dysphasia. *Nature* 344, 715, 19 April.

— (1990b) Feature-blindness: A case study. *Language Acquisition* 1, 139–64.

Gopnik, M. and Crago, M. (1991) Familial aggregation of a developmental language disorder. *Cognition* 39, 1–50.

Grimshaw, J. (1990) *Argument Structure*. Cambridge, MA: MIT Press.

Ingham, R. (1992) Syntactic input and verb transitivity. In R. Ingham and I. Phillipaki-Warburton (eds) *Working Papers in Linguistics*. Department of Linguistic Science, University of Reading.

Jakobson, R. (1968) *Child Language, Aphasia and Phonological Universals*. The Hague: Mouton.

Levinson, S. (1983) *Pragmatics*. Cambridge: Cambridge University Press.

Pinker, S. (1987) Resolving a learnability paradox in the acquisition of the verb lexicon. *Lexicon Project Working Papers* 17, 1–100. Cambridge, MA: MIT Centre for Cognitive Science.

— (1989) *Learnability and Cognition: The Acquisition of Argument Structure*. Cambridge, MA: MIT Press.

Quirk, R., Greenbaum, S., Leech, G. and Svartvik, J. (1985) *A Comprehensive Grammar of the English Language*. London: Longman.

2 Putting our Practice into Theory

DEBORAH CAMERON
University of Strathclyde

Introduction

It seems clear that the question of theory and practice touches a nerve for many applied linguists. Casting about for guidance on the duties of a keynote speaker, I began by looking back to last year's meeting as reported in the BAAL Spring newsletter, and was immediately confronted with Sue Blackwell's prophetic words: 'Perhaps', she concluded, 'next year's meeting will take us further towards the synthesis of theory and practice in Applied Linguistics which is still, for many of us, proving elusive' (Blackwell, 1992: 32).

Since the organisers chose 'evaluating theory and practice' as the theme for 1992, it seems they shared Sue Blackwell's hope. In their letter of invitation to me they listed a number of questions that might help to focus our thoughts on the matter, and I think it's worth repeating some of them.

(1) Applied linguistics presumably intends to be of use. How and to whom?
(2) How far can applied linguistic theory be evaluated and improved by confronting it with practical issues?
(3) Can applied linguistics be of use in evaluating practice, and if so how?

Taken together with Sue Blackwell's remarks, these questions suggest to me that we perceive some kind of general problem about the relation between theoretical and practical concerns. There's the sense of a gap or a disjunction between the two, and this causes a degree of anxiety about where we should locate ourselves — we are theorists but we also want to be 'of use'; we need to be 'confronted' with 'practical issues'; we want to be able to help practitioners 'evaluate' their practice. We are looking for a synthesis in which there would be a closer relationship between theory and practice, or at least a clearer model articulating what their relationship should be.

What catches my interest about this initially is not so much the questions themselves as our reasons for asking them. Why do we have this sense

15

of a problem, and what lies behind the anxiety? because I do think it's a widely shared feeling: indeed to some extent I share it myself.

Obviously, members of BAAL will differ in their views of the problem, and indeed in whether they perceive one. I am talking at the level of sweeping generalisations, ignoring the very important fact that applied linguists engage in all kinds of theoretical work which relate to very different sorts of practices outside the academy. 'The relationship between theory and practice' can ultimately only be specified on a case by case level, for it crucially depends on what sort of theory and more especially what practice you are talking about.

Nevertheless I think that as applied linguists we are collectively positioned, and perhaps even trapped, by a set of institutional and other discourses about theory and practice which are very general, in some ways rather contradictory, and which we do not fully control. These discourses propel us towards particular ways of understanding and talking about our own position, which in turn reinforce the polarisation of theory and practice. Let me try to unpack this rather obscure suggestion.

The Institutional Boundaries of Applied Linguistics

The question of what applied linguistics is, or what the term means, is a hardy perennial of occasions like this one down the years, and I won't presume to rehash the debate. But we all know 'applied linguistics' is a pretty elastic category, and that this elasticity has developed for institutional reasons. Speaking for myself, I can understand what I do as 'applied linguistics' only within a certain institutional discourse. This discourse is structured by two crucial assumptions: (1) that there is an autonomous discipline of linguistics; and (2) that within the boundaries of that discipline there is a subdivision into theoretical and applied linguistics. I may not find it easy or useful to draw those lines, but it is normative to draw them — as I am reminded every time I open the massive file in my office marked ESRC. And one of the criteria for drawing the line that divides 'theoretical' from 'applied' obviously has to do with the question of theory and practice.

This is not a simple question. The binary opposition 'theory vs. practice' is salient in a number of different discourses, but the relation between the two terms is a variable one. Let me mention two instances. First, there's a kind of everyday discourse in which theory is arcane and suspect, devalued by contrast with practice which is more grounded in common sense and the 'real world'. The clichés that circulate in this discourse are things like 'that's all very well in theory', the implication being that in practice it's irrelevant or unworkable. By contrast, there's a kind of academic discourse where 'theory' is accorded high status. Here there are alternative clichés, things like 'x's analysis is purely descriptive'. This implies the analysis doesn't advance theory; it therefore lacks a certain significance or value.

I don't want to suggest that any of us accepts either of these ways of talking uncritically, but I do think that as practitioners of an applied discipline we cannot be untouched by them. In particular, the fact that 'theory' and 'practice' come with different values attached to them is a problem for us. One obvious outcome — though not the only possible one — is to produce a hierarchy in which 'theoretical x', be it physics or linguistics, is seen as outranking 'applied x'. I say this isn't the only possible outcome, and I think it would be quite wrong to claim that most academics would endorse it. On the contrary I think most would dismiss it as vulgar nonsense. But resisting it often means deploying arguments from the same discourses of value.

One argument, for instance, says that applied disciplines are wrongly seen as purely practical, or as dependent on theories produced elsewhere. They make important theoretical contributions of their own. Certainly this is true of applied linguistics. But to say so is implicitly to accept the discourse that valorises theory and separates it from practice.

Another argument says that applied disciplines are particularly valuable *because* they are more relevant to 'real world concerns'. This argument is an appropriation of the everyday discourse where theory is conceived as arcane, irrelevant. The value judgements may be more subtle in this version, but they are nevertheless still present. In her report on last year's meeting, Joanna Channell glosses a point of view that she says 'found some favour' among participants:

> . . . when we work on real world issues, it is not theories which are of value, but rather the insights which we can derive because of our training as linguists. (Channell, 1992: 32)

As I read this, it recapitulates the notion of a gap between theories and 'real world issues', implying that the former are not, in this context, of value.

Let me make clear what bothers me about all this. I am not primarily concerned to dispute the substance of the arguments themselves. It's the framework within which they serve any purpose that I have reservations about. This framework not only separates theory and practice, the ivory tower and the real world, axiomatically; it actually sets them against one another. No wonder a synthesis is 'proving elusive' if the claims of one term have conventionally to be pressed by downgrading the claims of the other.

My reservations about this and my feeling that it's a trap are heightened within the current academic political climate in this country. Researchers are caught between on one hand, being judged on criteria of immediate practical utility in the 'real world' and on the other, the sort of hierarchical prestige judgements embodied in the idea 'selectivity'. I am troubled by the idea that a government intent on under-resourcing education, on limiting the freedom of academics and circumscribing their influence, may be able to capitalise on oppositions and divisions already established among ourselves.

Or let's consider a rather different case, one perhaps closer to the theme of this conference and the experience of this audience: the debate on English teaching in the National Curriculum of England and Wales. My own view of what happened, though I know not all colleagues share it, is that linguists took a beating. Our representatives made headway in the committee rooms, but in the media and other arenas of public opinion I think we were pilloried. I'll say more about this later on; but here I want to point out that our opponents were able to exploit the discursively-constructed opposition between head-in-the-clouds know-nothing theoreticians and 'real world concerns' about educational standards, literacy and equality of opportunity. In this instance, we ended up being placed on the wrong side of the rhetorical fence.

So far I've been arguing, I hope not too incomprehensibly, that we need to be wary of the way theory versus practice is set up as a binary opposition and a hierarchy of value. For us as applied linguists this becomes especially complicated and difficult, because we are positioned ambiguously: in our relations with other linguists we get identified with the 'practical', while in our relations with practitioners outside the academy, and with public opinion, we get identified with 'theory'. Given the rhetorical and institutional power of the opposition, the task of synthesis looks daunting indeed. I wonder if we might not be better off trying to deconstruct the opposition.

Deconstructing the Opposition between Theory and Practice

Within the framework that's been most significant in forming the way I think — a particular kind of feminism — the relationship between theory and practice is conceived rather differently. The terms are not treated as opposites or even as separate and complementary, but as always co-present and mutually implicated. Thus any form of what we call 'practice' must inevitably include 'theory': common sense is a theory, distinguished from other theories, if at all, only by the degree of formality and self-consciousness with which it is invoked. When someone purports to criticise or 'go beyond' common sense, they are not putting theory where previously there was none, but replacing one theory with another.

There again, since all knowledge is made, and must inevitably be made, from some or other point of view, even the most formal and self-consciously constructed theory cannot be detached from the practices, histories, circumstances and beliefs of those who produced it. Theory-making is itself a social practice in the 'real world'.

For feminists, this way of looking at theory and practice is partly a critical lever that enables us to take issue with the androcentricity of much canonical knowledge — the central point being that knowledge is not disinterested. But of course it also entails that our own attempts at producing knowledge cannot be disinterested either. The aim of producing knowledge has therefore to be reconceived: rather than being a quest for objective universal truths, it has to become something more reflexive, more grounded in the desire to construct particular, and no doubt limited understandings of particular activities and their meaning for particular people. That is roughly what I mean by the phrase 'putting our practice into theory': a process of critical reflection on the activities through which we make meaning in our lives, which is also a practice of making new meanings.

Verbal Hygiene

Recently, I've become interested in a set of activities which I refer to collectively as 'verbal hygiene'. As the term implies, the activities I'm interested in are to do with regulating language, cleaning it up, improving it; they include not only the complex of regulative activities linguists have discussed under the heading of prescriptivism, but also many activities we have paid far less attention to: things like campaigning for the use of plain language on official forms, advocating spelling reform, dialect preservation or artificial languages, taking courses or reading self-help literature about assertiveness, better conversation, the gentle art of verbal self-defence, editing prose in conformity with a house style, producing guidelines on politically-correct language, regulating the talk of committees in accordance with parliamentary procedure, regulating the use of swear words in the media or the workplace. These activities are not linked by any one political perspective or view of language. They are linked, however, by a very strong concern with value. Verbal hygiene comes into being when people reflect on language in a critical, in the sense of evaluative, way; and though I have chosen to look at activities where this evaluative impulse has been more or less institutionalised, the impulse itself, I would argue, is far more general and pervasive. One way of defining verbal hygiene might be as 'the popular culture of language'.

Now you might wonder why I should consider this work on verbal hygiene relevant to a conference on evaluating theory and practice in applied linguistics. I agree the links are not obvious, but this is how I would make them.

First, nothing I have said about deconstructing the discursive opposition between theory and practice necessarily invalidates the sense of a problem I began with, the sense that there is some gap, some disjunction between the sort of work we do and the 'real world concerns' we would like it to address. I think it is misleading to gloss this as a gap between theory and practice *per se*; but it might be worth exploring the notion of a rather different sort of gap between the concerns of linguists and the concerns of people who aren't linguists, when it comes to thinking and talking about language. This gap, I suggest, is constituted by very different attitudes to questions of *value*.

I can illustrate the point with the following story. About ten years ago, I was walking through Bloomsbury when I noticed a handlettered poster advertising an exhibition in the Conway Hall titled 'The use and abuse of language'. I was curious, I wasn't in a hurry, so I went along to have a look at it.

It turned out to be an amateurish looking set of display boards on which newspaper cuttings were pinned up with commentary in the spirit of George Orwell. In front of the display were formica tables where you could talk to the organisers, pick up a leaflet setting out the aims of their organisation and add your name to their mailing list. One of the organisers asked me what I thought of the display. I said it was very interesting, and added — probably so he wouldn't mistake me for a crank like himself — that my interest was professional since I was a linguist. Immediately his face lit up. 'How marvellous', he said, 'An expert on the subject. Do tell me what linguists are doing to combat the abuse of language'. Not knowing what to say, I made my excuses and left.

Linguists' Attitudes to Evaluative Responses to Language

This chance encounter now seems to me a perfect illustration of the vast gulf that seems to exist between what interests linguists about language and what interests everyone else about it. The simplest way to describe this is that most people's primary way of reflecting on linguistic issues is an *evaluative* one: is it right or wrong, good or bad, beautiful or ugly, used or abused? Whereas linguists undergo a process of professional socialisation designed to get rid of the evaluative reflex, or at least to mute it. The cardinal rule that linguistics is 'descriptive not prescriptive' is what constitutes us as experts. Paradoxically, however, it also makes it more difficult for us to engage in discussion beyond the boundaries of our discipline about matters where our expertise might be relevant and useful. I believe this was one of the reasons for the apparent inability of linguists to sway the public debate on English teaching: many of us, and I include myself, were reluctant to get involved in talk about norms, rules, standards and values. The authoritarians of the Pro-grammar Right had no such reluctance; their way of talking meshed with the concerns of the Man in the Conway Hall.

Now, one response to this might well be to point out that the conservative faction, represented by such intellectual luminaries as Norman Tebbit and Prince Charles, were talking bigoted rubbish. If most people are more receptive to bigoted rubbish than to reasoned argument based on sound empirical evidence, that is unfortunate; but it is surely no part of the expert linguist's job to pander to ignorance and prejudice. Indeed not, I quite agree. It is absolutely right to oppose the particular values conservatives championed during the grammar furore. But there seems to be a feeling that to be concerned with linguistic norms, to admit any connection between the spheres of language and morality, value or aesthetics, is in itself authoritarian; and that, I think, is not obviously right.

In his recent book, *Linguistic Variation and Change*, James Milroy has argued that linguists are generally in a muddle about the concept of normativity, which we wrongly equate with authoritarian prescriptivism. Milroy states firmly that 'all language descriptions, no matter how objective they are, must be normative . . . because to be accurate they have to coincide with the consensus norms of the community concerned' (Milroy, 1992: 8–9). He goes on to make a distinction between 'norm-enforcing', which is what prescriptivists do, and 'norm-observing', which is what linguists do even if they don't acknowledge it.

I am grateful to Milroy for his clear recognition that language using is fundamentally a normative practice — linguists can always use a reminder that what they study is not a natural phenomenon — but I don't think he follows his own argument to its logical conclusion. The distinction between 'observing norms' — that is, objectively describing what they are — and enforcing them — that is, suggesting they constitute the 'right' way to do things — is not, in practice, very easy to maintain, particularly for linguists who want their work to be 'of use' to people outside the discipline; because people whose approach to language is basically evaluative have a tendency to treat norm-observing statements as norm-enforcing ones. A very obvious example is that most people regard modern dictionaries, which present themselves as works of descriptive lexicography, as absolute authorities on the provenance and meaning of words.

Another example is the mini-industry of verbal hygiene for professional women that has sprung up in the last few years, generating courses, training manuals, self-help literature and a growing army of expert consultants. The materials produced by this industry are clearly and identifiably based on scholarly findings from the field of language and gender: but the observations of scholars have been turned into advice. Where the linguist says that women differ from men in having a tendency to use indirect requests rather than imperatives, the training manual says: 'speak directly when making requests of male subordinates. Women shy away from giving blatant orders, but men find the indirect approach manipulative and confusing'.

Some linguists might see this sort of thing as simply a misuse of scholarly research, a grafting on of questionable value judgements to accounts which deliberately avoided them. I do not think matters are so simple.

In the history of our discipline we have too often treated normative activities like making judgements about right and wrong, good and bad, as an alien growth perversely grafted onto language-using and not something intrinsic to it. But it could be argued, to the contrary, that this judging and meddling and tinkering must be built into any workable communication system. Because communicating is a social, public act, it must be carried on with reference to norms, and these in turn must be able to become the subject of overt comment. When one speaker's utterance invites another's response — and presumably this is a basic design feature of human languages — the possibility is always open that the response will focus on the norms for linguistic performance itself.

The other point on which I would take issue with Milroy is his assumption that the norms linguists deal with are paradigmatically what he calls 'consensus norms'. Certainly the study of verbal hygiene suggests that many linguistic norms are highly contested matters, and that the outcome of dispute about them is rarely best described as a consensus. This again is something social scientists have not always been very attentive to. As the psychologist Michael Billig has said, we

> often tend to assume that the essential aspect of rules lies in the fact that rules are followed. Yet there is an equally important, but sometimes neglected aspect to rules: namely that rules arise from and themselves give rise to arguments. (Billig, 1991: 50)

I believe that making value judgements about language is both an intrinsic part of using it and an inevitable consequence of theorising about it. To say that is not to endorse any specific judgement, or any particular set of values; as Michael Billig observes, there is always room for arguments about what rules, norms and values we should espouse. If there is a place in society at large for the insights of applied linguistics to be 'of use', it has to be negotiated by way of engaging in those arguments.

Conclusion

Many of us here today probably do see our work as in some sense concerned with what the Man in the Conway Hall referred to as 'combatting the abuse of language'. We do see examples of deplorable ignorance and prejudice in certain commonplace ways of using language and certain popular views on the subject; and we feel some obligation to contest these ways of talking. In order to do this successfully, I believe we must look beyond the particularities of what people are saying, and give weight to the more general allegiance it exemplifies, a deep commitment to the discourse of value. This discourse has a moral dimension that touches on deep desires and fears, such as the desire for order, or the fear of uncertainty and fragmentation. Our training as linguists makes language a much less potent symbol for us. But even if we cannot share the passions and the pleasures of verbal hygiene, it is a practice we should take seriously by putting it into our theories about the nature and significance of language in use.

References

Billig, M. (1991) *Ideology and Opinions*. London: Sage.
Blackwell, S. (1992) Conference report. *BAAL Newsletter*. Spring 1992, 31–2.
Channell, J. (1992) Conference report. *BAAL Newsletter*. Spring 1992, 32–3.
Milroy, J. (1992) *Linguistic Variation and Change*. Oxford: Blackwell.

3 Applied Linguistics as Evaluation of Theory and Practice: (Inter)Relating the Problems of Learners, Teachers and Therapists

MARTIN BYGATE and CAROLYN LETTS
University of Reading

Introduction

Applied linguistics is often thought of (notably by teachers) as having a theoretical vocation. The purpose of this paper is to suggest rather that applied linguistics is an activity whose function is to relate theories to professional practices, and to do so in the interests of professional practitioners as well as theoreticians. There may well be implications arising from this view regarding the nature and ownership of (and participation in) applied language research. This paper, however, focuses on the issue of how applied linguistics can match theoretical interests to professional problems.

We start from a recent definition of applied linguistics:

> the theoretical and empirical study of real-world problems in which language is a central factor. (Brumfit, 1991: 46)

This definition implies that applied linguistics is not a single activity — it may be either theoretical or empirical. Theoretical activity presumably involves investigation of features of normal and abnormal language use in terms of conceivable descriptive frameworks (e.g. Green & Hecht, 1989; Lennon, 1992 for descriptions of learners' errors, or Crystal, Fletcher & Garman, 1989 for description of children's pathological speech/language difficulties), or potential explanations (e.g. errors being due to competing automations, or to conceptual/perceptual difficulties, as exemplified in language pathology by Tallal & Piercy, 1978; Chiat & Hirson, 1987). This is essentially conceptual research aiming at producing heuristic or descriptive devices. A large body of applied linguistic publications in recent years represents this type of concern, particularly in the area of language teaching (e.g. Allwright, 1984; Brumfit, 1984; Widdowson, 1978, 1983; Wilkins, 1976).

A commonly perceived limitation of such work is that it often does not aim to operationalise terminology or provide empirical verification. This may be the inevitable cost of conceptual creativity. To expect the contrary would be rather like expecting all departments of architectural design to be equally concerned with material feasibility. Designers may for instance develop categories which turn out not to be reliably applicable, at least within current technology. One applied language example might be Widdowson's 1983 notions of the territorial and co-operative principles, for which diagnostic criteria are not self-evident. Diagnostic criteria are equally elusive, however, in discourse analysis (for instance, in the definitions of Sinclair & Couthard's, 1975 list of 'acts'), and in accounts of conceivable explanations in critical linguistics (for instance, the criterial evidence supporting the assertion that the use of the passive in certain newspaper texts is ideologically motivated (e.g. Kress, 1991)). The point is that while applied linguistics involves identifying what we think we know about language in use and development, it also has to address the status of this knowledge, that is, answer the question 'how do we know this?' This is where empirical research intrudes. For it is empirical research which can serve to test out the strengths and weaknesses of conceptual frameworks.

However, questions are not only to be asked of conceptual research. Empirical work cannot on its own be relied upon to be systematic or valid: descriptions require principled taxonomies, which relate aspects of events to underlying interpretations. That is, for the descriptive enterprise to be possible, applied linguistics needs reliable and valid frameworks.

Hence, the application of frameworks of analysis serves simultaneously to describe data, and to validate the instruments of description. There is then a sense in which there is a mutual dependency between theoretical and empirical study, and this can be defined as a three-way dependency: theoretical descriptions are in need of empirical data for validation and improvement; empirical data (for instance the data familiar to speech/language therapists and teachers) is in need of systematic description for overt and underlying regularities to be perceived. The third dependency is that, to be operative, the activity of empirical description itself requires both relevant data and carefully developed theoretical frameworks. This can be summarised as in Figure 1.

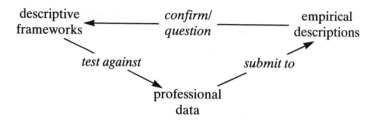

Figure 1 Relationship between theoretical and empirical study

In this perspective, a major potential outcome of the cycle is the revision or confirmation of the framework. Yet this account fails to consider the function of responding to real-world problems. The diagram therefore needs modifying:

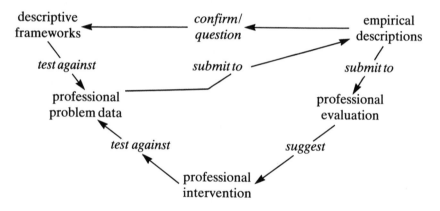

Figure 2 Relationship between theoretical and empirical study: taking account of real-world problems

Figure 2 indicates how problem data can emerge from the context of professional intervention. It also shows how findings emerging from the application of descriptive frameworks are not merely subjected to descriptive evaluation, but are open to evaluation by professionals interested in exploring possible professional intervention. New intervention strategies can then be formulated in order to attempt to address the original problem. Feedback from this development can be obtained through fresh descriptions and submitted once again to further professional evaluation. (This resembles Popper's cycle: problem → tentative theory → error elimination (1976: 132).)

From this background discussion we turn to consider how a specific applied linguistics issue can provide information to help the development both of descriptive frameworks, and of intervention procedures.

Theory and Practice in Speech/Language Therapy and Language Teaching

The real-world problem of interest in this section is the effect of intervention on language ability — L1 language ability, where the speech/language therapist is concerned; L2 language ability where the teacher is concerned. Conceptualising this in terms of theory and practice, the teacher/therapist can be conceived of as being the theoretician — hypothesising the nature of the problem, and then hypothesising the preferred intervention. At the same time the therapy client's/learner's developing responses can be conceived of as the practical outcomes:

theory > practice ::

teacher/therapist > (intervention → learners'/clients' responses)

In this view, the teacher/therapist (T/T) is engaged in two levels of operation and four stages of professional activity:

Stage 1
Level: theoretical: T/T
          — diagnoses a problem for the client/learner
          — focuses on a potentially desirable area for intervention

Stage 2
Level: theoretical: T/T
          — selects potentially effective types of intervention in light of the need

Stage 3
Level: practical: T/T
          — implements the selected mode of intervention
          — elicits language activity from the client/learner

Stage 4
Level: theoretical/practical: T/T
          — observes the language activity immediately/over time
          — assesses the efficacy of the intervention used
          — returns to Stage 1

For the teacher/therapist, the problem is practical, i.e. enabling the client/learner to enrich her/his linguistic repertoire and/or mastery over it.

Any diagnosed problem, however, is only a hypothetical construct: specialists (and others involved) may be wrong. The tentative theory is a putative solution. Error elimination occurs when the therapist/teacher discovers that the diagnosis and/or intervention were in some way mistaken.

A comment is needed, however. The teacher/therapist is operating at *two* levels of theory: firstly, that of the particular problem of a given client/ learner, and the attempt to solve it; and secondly that of relations between a wide range of *potential* problems and of a possibly equally wide range of *potential* solutions. In other words, *two* kinds of problem-solving are going on simultaneously: that of the problem(s) of actual subjects; and that of developing a wider understanding of the kinds of problems subjects may have, and an increasingly discriminating understanding of ways and means of dealing with them. We are arguing that this second level of understanding is the level at which professional progress is gradually being made.

To summarise, we are making two points we consider important. First, unless applied linguists try out their theories in practice, they will not be able to improve their theories, either of the nature of language users' problems, or of the nature of professional intervention. However, we are *also* arguing that unless therapists and teachers are able to carefully observe and evaluate the effects of intervention, we are very unlikely to learn very much about our practice(s). The real-world problem at issue here is that of professional development. In the next section of this paper we illustrate our argument with two examples, one from speech/language therapy and one from language teaching.

Illustration 1: Speech/Language Therapy

The example and discussion in this section will be taken from speech/ language therapy with children, although many of the problems and proposed solutions are relevant to work with language impaired adults (e.g. adults who have suffered brain-damage) as well.

The speech and language therapist sees children who have communication deficits affecting the acquisition of both first and any subsequent languages. The task facing the therapist is to locate as quickly and accurately as possible the areas of deficit and to apply appropriate remediation. Such deficits will frequently be linguistic in nature, although it is recognised that deficits in pragmatics and in non-verbal communication may also occur. In order to work effectively, the therapist is expected to draw on available knowledge about normal language development in children. With mono-

lingual English-speaking children at least, this pool of knowledge is extensive and wide-ranging, and is available in the form of checklists, profiles or
standardised tests, all of which provide the therapist with some sort of comparison of the language-disordered with the 'normal' child. This idealised
picture of the 'normal' language acquirer is perhaps comparable with the
idealised linguistic description or grammar of a foreign language, in that it is
the norm to which the learner aspires. In the case of first language remediation, however, due account must be taken of the child's own dialect.

In addition, diagnosis involves weighing up environmental and constitutional influences on language development, and also comparing the
nature and degree of deficit across different areas of the child's linguistic system; comparisons are thus made externally, i.e. with other children, and
internally, within the child. Remediation needs are identified by focusing on
those parts of the child's linguistic system that are particularly impaired in
relation to both the norm and in relation to the child's other linguistic skills.
In addition, while unfortunately less thought may be given to the child's
wider social and cultural needs, careful attention is paid to the demands of
formal education, especially with older children.

Once areas of deficit/need have been identified, the next step is to
devise remediation. Therapy activities are ideally tailor-made to the child's
needs; the therapist will draw on published materials and adapt them
accordingly, but there is also a strong tradition within speech/language
therapy of constructing materials and improvising with toys, in order to
devise tasks that pinpoint particular skills.

This complex diagnostic approach, plus the matching of remedial tasks
to individual needs, may seem a luxury when contrasted with the second language classroom where greater numbers will need to be taught language
together, often during a circumscribed period of time. However, speech and
language therapists nowadays are subject to the need to justify and evaluate
their work; this means that time cannot be wasted as a result of failure to
accurately pinpoint areas of breakdown, or as a result of non-targeted
therapy (see CSLT, *Communicating Quality*, 1991). Careful evaluation of
the remediation process not only helps the individual case, but feeds into
wider knowledge regarding types of disorder and appropriate remediation.
Thus the theoretical basis for therapy is also enhanced.

Case illustration: R.

The points made above can be illustrated with an account of how this
diagnostic process was carried out with one language-disordered child, R.
R., aged 5 years 4 months, was referred to Reading University's Linguistic

Assessment Clinic (LAC). Prior to this referral, R.'s problems with language were ill-defined; one report spoke of 'specific but mild difficulties with processing language'. Parental concern focused on problems with retaining new vocabulary and speech problems, in that her speech was hard to understand at times.

The procedure at LAC is to run the assessment over two sessions, usually a week apart, and each about 45–60 minutes long. In the first session, relatively non-specific procedures are carried out, and a language sample is taken (the whole session is video- and audio-recorded). On the basis of trends which emerge in the first session, hypotheses are formulated about the nature of the problem, and these are explored through the use of more specific probes in the course of session two (see also Fletcher, this volume, on this process).

During the first assessment session, it was initially difficult to locate any problems at all in R.'s ability to communicate. She interacted appropriately for her age with the therapist who conducted the session and her spontaneous utterances showed complex syntax, although with some immaturities. The following examples illustrate this:

(1) (talking of her younger sister) 'when Mummy's gonna collect her, she's gonna collect her lunchbox from nursery'
(2) (explaining her absence from school) 'I'm not there because, you see, I'm here'
(3) (somewhat more muddled) 'I went to school with a packed lunches, and have a picnic outside'

Furthermore, a standardised test of language comprehension (Reynell Verbal Comprehension Scale, Second Revision, Reynell & Huntley, 1985) suggested that she was only slightly under the average for her age.

However, R. did perform very poorly on a formal test of word finding, (German, 1989) involving naming pictured objects and actions. Sometimes she was able to compensate by paraphrasing (e.g. *microphone* = 'talking thing'), but some of her responses were bizarre (e.g. *weighing* = 'see how heavy his feet are'). It was also noted that R. had marked difficulties in repeating back words given to her by the therapist.

On the basis of this first session it became clear that R. had problems associated with vocabulary, at least when it came to producing appropriate lexical items. The following hypotheses were formulated:

(1) R. has word-retrieval difficulties; that is to say, she has problems accessing or producing vocabulary items that she nevertheless understands. If this is the case, she should perform much better on a test of vocabulary comprehension, than on naming tasks.

(2) R.'s lexical semantic system is disordered, with the result that she assigns the wrong meanings to words, and says things that sound 'odd'.
(3) R. has auditory processing problems, so that she is unable to adequately perceive or store the phonological forms of new words. This is suggested by her problems in repeating. Young children are known to normally acquire new lexical forms rapidly, after minimal exposure. This is commonly referred to as 'fast mapping', as described for example by Dollaghan, 1985, and Rice, Buhr & Nemeth, 1990. This accounts for the vast growth in vocabulary that occurs in early childhood. Dollaghan found in a later study (Dollaghan, 1987) that language impaired children have more problems than normal in reproducing recently heard new words, although their performance is comparable to normals on the comprehension of such words. It is possible that R.'s ability to acquire vocabulary is impeded by inadequate auditory discrimination, memory and storage.

The second assessment session in fact showed hypothesis 3 to be the most accurate. A standardised test of vocabulary comprehension (Dunn, Dunn, Leola, Whetton & Pintilie, 1982), revealed that she has major problems in this area as well as with vocabulary production, so that her difficulties are not limited to word-retrieval. A non-standardised procedure to probe semantic association revealed no problems. Other probes, however, showed up major problems with auditory discrimination and with auditory memory (digit span); she was performing well below age-norm in these areas. Repetition of nonsense words was unsuccessful if they involved more than two syllables, as illustrated by the following examples:

(1) /basuna/ was reproduced firstly as [basusa], and secondly, [basɔsa].
(2) /ganɔvei/ was reproduced firstly as [gafɔvei], and secondly, [garavei].

Recommended therapy for R. then would be directed at improving her auditory perceptual skills, and applying these skills to the acquisition of new vocabulary. Teaching of new vocabulary in the absence of attention to her auditory processing abilities would be unlikely to succeed.

It can thus be seen how a detailed assessment procedure resulted in the targeting of therapy for this child. As already stated, this was made possible by the availability of knowledge regarding normal language acquisition, as well as looking at the overall profile of strengths and weaknesses displayed by the child. While environmental and constitutional factors have to be taken into account, this is usually a process of looking out for and 'excluding' such factors. If these factors are not present, the child is assumed to start out from the same point as any other, and hence comparison to the 'norm' is valid and informative in focusing later probes.

Illustration 2: Second Language Learning

The illustration from speech/language therapy demonstrates a trial and error procedure at two points, those of diagnosis and of intervention. Thus the individual case serves to develop professional expertise at both points. It does this with reference to normative data and to the child's individual profile. With second language learners, any approach that relies on 'norms' is much more problematical, given that learners will vary enormously in terms of cultural, educational and first language experience. For second language teachers, however, much of value could be obtained from looking at profiles of strengths and weaknesses within individuals. In language teaching, teachers tend not to work with individual cases. However, in principle the possibilities of developing diagnosis and intervention may be rather similar. Once individuals have been profiled, they could then possibly be grouped into types for purposes of teaching. In this part of the section, we consider how individuals' strengths and weaknesses might be identified for individuals and groups of second language learners. We then show how tasks can be analysed in order to ascertain in which linguistic areas they promote practice and learning.

Let us take the case of the speech of a Taiwanese speaker of English. Analysis of parts of a recording shows that his language varies considerably in fluency, accuracy, and structural complexity:

Table 1 Speech characteristics of a Taiwanese speaker of English in two contexts

Topic	Ex. 1 (95 words) Reasons for study	Ex. 2 (132 words) Description of own room
Silent pauses	8	24
Filled pauses	2	14
Backtracks	2	10
Incomplete clauses	1	5
Mean clause length	10.1	6.4
Full clauses	7	9
Errors	6	3

It is not necessary to carry out a statistical test to show that the figures demonstrate a striking difference in incidence of: markers of disfluency; incomplete clauses; clause length; and error. Extract 1 on these measures is far more fluent (longer clauses, fewer disfluent markers) although it does contain more errors. On one topic, then, the same speaker is more fluent and syntactically developed than on another. This is not an unusual finding (cf. for instance Ellis, 1987; Selinker & Douglas, 1985).

The literature suggests several possible diagnoses of this speaker's performances, but we will consider two. Firstly, using Selinker & Douglas' terminology, the speaker has reasonable familiarity with one 'discourse domain' and virtually none with the other. The evidence for this view is that in the second extract, after much disfluency, the speaker eventually manages to produce a relatively fluent five clause description of his room in the last 40 words (i.e. in the final 30% of the recording). This explanation then might rely on the notion that knowledge of an underlying schema may account for differences in language performance. There are potential implications for language teaching in this diagnosis.

An alternative and more economical explanation is that the speaker has a basic *syntactic* fluency (as indicated by his performance in extract 1), but has vocabulary-related problems in the second extract (signalled by increased pausing around the points of lexical accessing, more incomplete clauses, as well as shorter clauses). Looking closer, two kinds of vocabulary problem can be diagnosed. Firstly, the speaker clearly *knows* sufficient vocabulary (he eventually manages to complete the task). In this area he may well have problems in *accessing* vocabulary. However, a second type of vocabulary problem can also be diagnosed from the disfluent 70% of the recording, namely the speaker's apparent lack of *strategies* for dealing smoothly with the problem, as evidenced by the many incomplete clauses. All three diagnoses can lead to different kinds of suggestion for pedagogic intervention. It is worth pointing out that such a fine-grained approach to diagnosing learners' difficulties is unusual in most teaching situations.

The point to be made here is that the use of different communicative tasks can help to diagnose the individual's problems, but can also help to contribute to a more general picture of language proficiency. The question then arises how to bring about the potentially relevant improvement for the learner.

In a separate study, one of the authors (Bygate, 1988) studied the language produced by non-native speakers working on five well-known classroom communication activities. Here we will consider just one of the five exercises, a task modelled along the lines of '20 questions'. This task is often recommended for practising the use of questions and for developing general fluency. Study of the incidence of language features shows one or two interesting findings. Compared with other tasks, this one gave rise to:

(1) Comparatively short non-finite utterances
(2) a relatively high type–token ratio
(3) a high incidence of question forms
(4) an even distribution of turns within the group.

While these findings confirm the relevance of the exercise for practising question forms (feature 3), features 1, 2 and 4 suggest that the exercise might also be useful for practising lexical fluency. A high type–token ratio suggests that the talk uses a relatively varied vocabulary; short non-finite utterances suggests low grammatical complexity, that is, greater emphasis on lexis than on grammar. Point 4 indicates that the exercise tends to enable all members of a group to get practice. Taken together the three features point to a potentially salient aspect of language practice. Furthermore, within the exercise there are possibilities for varying the amount of recycling of lexical items — by controlling more or less tightly the topic range of the items (e.g. industrial products, animal species, towns, etc.).

To continue the parallel with the procedures followed under speech/language therapy, it would now be necessary to apply the practice task to see whether this would help students, such as the Taiwanese student discussed earlier, to mobilise and extend their range of active vocabulary. Typically, this has not in fact been carried out. However, it could be argued that a responsible pedagogy needs to adopt an evaluative stance in respect of such tasks, and hence, implement the task to see its effect.

An alternative diagnosis of the problem (for instance, difficulties in discourse domain, or weaknesses in the use of communication strategies) might give rise to suggestions of other specific practice tasks capable of developing the speaker's ability to handle, say, descriptions, or to use a range of communication strategies. In each case, improved appreciation of intervention procedures can be gained by evaluating the efficacy of each activity type on the learner's development. This is a relatively neglected aspect of applied linguistic work in language teaching, and one deserving more attention.

Conclusion

Applied linguistics as defined by Brumfit above (1991) is seen as *problem-oriented*. The essence of this definition is that the discipline is concerned not principally with the description of states of affairs, but with an enquiry into ways in which states of affairs can be altered by professional awareness and intervention. Its relevance is not merely to improve understanding of language acquisition: it is also to improve intervention, and maintain and promote a professional concern for real-world issues. In order to do this, and to be seen to be doing it, it may be worthwhile for applied linguists to give a higher profile to an evaluative stance with respect to the effects of their theories on the real world. To do this effectively of course requires time and money. Perhaps this is something for BAAL to pay attention to in the coming 25 years.

References

Allwright, R. L. (1984) The importance of interaction in classroom language learning. *Applied Linguistics* 5, 2.

Brumfit, C. J. (1979) 'Communicative' language teaching: An educational perspective. In C. J. Brumfit and K. Johnson (eds) *The Communicative Approach to Language Teaching*. Oxford: OUP.

— (1984) *Communicative Methodology in Language Teaching*. Cambridge: CUP.

— (1988) Applied linguistics and communicative language teaching. *Annual Review of Applied Linguistics* Vol. 8, 1987. Cambridge: CUP.

— (1991) Applied linguistics in higher education: Riding the storm. *BAAL Newsletter* 38, 45–9.

Bygate, M. (1988) Linguistic and strategic features in the language of learners on oral communication exercises. Unpublished PhD thesis, Institute of Education, University of London.

Chiat, S. and Hirson, A. (1987) From conceptual intention to utterance: A study of impaired language output in a child with developmental dysphasia. *British Journal of Disorders of Communication* 22, 37–64.

College of Speech and Language Therapists (1991) Professional standards for speech and language therapists. *Communicating Quality*. London: College of Speech and Language Therapists.

Crystal, D., Fletcher, P. and Garman, M. (1989) *Grammatical Analysis of Language Disability* (2nd edn). London: Whurr.

Dollaghan, C. A. (1985) Child meets word: 'Fast mapping' in preschool children. *Journal of Speech and Hearing Research* 28, 449–54.

— (1987) Fast mapping in normal and language impaired children. *Journal of Speech and Hearing Disorders* 52, 218–22.

Dunn, L. M., Dunn, Leola M., Whetton, C. and Pintilie, D. (1982) *British Picture Vocabulary Scale*. Windsor: NFER-Nelson.

Ellis, R. (ed.) (1987) *Second Language Acquisition in Context*. Englewood, Cliffs: Prentice Hall.

German, D. J. (1989) *Test of Word Finding*. Leicester: DLM.

Green, P. S. and Hecht, K. (1989) Investigating learners language. In C. J. Brumfit and R. Mitchell (eds) *Research in the Language Classroom*. ELT DOLS 133, MEP in association with the British Council.

Kress, G. (1991) Cultural considerations in linguistic description. Keynote talk, BAAL Annual Meeting, University of Durham.

Lennon, P. (1991) Error: Some problems of definition, identification and distinction. *Applied Linguistics* 12, 2.

Popper, K. (1976) *Unended Quest* (p. 132). Glasgow: Fontana/Collins.

Reynell, J. and Huntley, M. (1985) *Reynell Developmental Language Scales* (2nd Revision). Windsor: NFER-Nelson.

Rice, M. L., Buhr, J. C. and Nemeth, M. (1990) Fast mapping word-learning abilities of language-delayed preschoolers. *Journal of Speech and Hearing Disorders*.

Selinker, L. and Douglas, D. (1985) Wrestling with context in interlanguage theory. *Applied Linguistics* 6, 2.

Sinclair, J. McH. and Coulthard (1975) *Towards an Analysis of Discourse*. Oxford: OUP.

Tallal, P. and Piercy, M. (1978) Defects of auditory perception in children with developmental dysphasia. In M. A. Wyke (ed.) *Developmental Dysphasia*. London: Academic Press.

Widdowson, H. G. (1978) *Teaching Language as Communication*. Oxford: OUP.

— (1983) *Learning Purpose and Language Use*. Oxford: OUP.

Wilkins, D. A. (1976) *Notional Syllabuses*. Oxford: OUP.

4 Writing in Another Culture: The Value of Students' KAL in Writing Pedagogy

SIMON PARDOE
University of Lancaster

Introduction

This paper reports part of a case study into the experiences of six bilingual students meeting the demands of factual writing in Standard English on an access course in an inner city Further Education College. Through retrospective interviews about specific examples of course writing, the study explores the implicit and explicit knowledge and perceptions about language, texts and processes of writing that students brought to, and developed during, their writing. The findings give a sense of the sophistication of the thinking and writing practices of the students, and of the problems and frustrations they faced. I will suggest that their thinking and even the problems they experienced form a potentially valuable resource for further learning.

My motivation for the study was to look again, with newly acquired insights from linguistic theory, at the kind of teaching of writing that I had been involved in prior to studying applied linguistics. I make this point because if I seem critical of what I found it is with full recognition that this was my own practice. This suggests to me that teachers working with enormous thought and commitment can still miss valuable teaching opportunities if we do not have the benefit of recent theoretical perspectives from applied linguistics and the opportunity to research our own teaching.

The findings here show that a text produced by a student and viewed as unsuccessful by the tutor does not necessarily demonstrate a lack of 'skills'. In their thinking about their texts, these students made important decisions based on their implicit or explicit construction of the communicative purpose of their text, and on their previously successful writing strategies. Yet

37

these decisions were not recognised, and not affirmed or disaffirmed, by the tutor's assessment. Because the students were writing within a different cultural context their decisions also frequently appeared to be at odds with the (implicit) assumptions and expectations of the tutor.

Aims

A theoretical perspective which is central to this study is the view of language as social semiotic (Halliday, 1989a), together with an associated recognition of the genre-specific requirements of written texts for acceptance by 'discourse communities' (see Swales, 1990). These perspectives reveal the inadequacy of seeing surface compliance with standardised grammar and spelling as the qualities that make a text 'successful'. Yet they also reveal the inadequacy of constructs that I have used in criteria for assessment such as 'clarity for the reader' and 'appropriacy', since these also do not identify explicitly for students the nature of the teacher's cultural and genre-specific expectations of their text.

This raised the question for me of how bilingual students from other cultures conceive, and manage to meet, the genre-specific demands made on their own written texts in an educational context in the UK. Of particular concern was how they may do so in the absence of the 'guided text analysis' advocated in recent teaching literature (Carter, 1990; Swales, 1990).

In recognition of the complexity of texts, writers in *Knowledge about Language and the Curriculum: The LINC Reader* (Carter, 1990) propose the pedagogic view that 'knowledge about language' (KAL) cannot simply be taught, but that students already possess considerable KAL, either implicitly or explicitly. This KAL can provide the basis for further learning through reflection on (and discursive analysis of) students' existing competence.

In terms of bilingual students with a variety of very different educational backgrounds (see Bourne, 1989; Raimes, 1987), this raised a question for me of whether such students' knowledge about English texts in a UK cultural context can be sufficient (and sufficiently shared) to provide the basis for such an approach.

In exploring these questions it was not the intention to produce a fair or representative account of the course. As I shall explain below, my research method actually brought to the fore students' more problematic experiences of the course. I focused also on students' writing processes, but will not discuss this in detail here.

The context

Because this is a case study of individual writers writing particular texts and revealing KAL in relation to these, it is important first to describe the context and the writers. The students' course was a BTEC First Diploma in Business Studies (BTEC = Business & Technical Education Council). The Diploma is considered equivalent to four GCSEs at C+ for entry to Higher Education. BTEC courses are developed in consultation with employers and include at least some work experience. Students are assessed predominantly in terms of their demonstration of skills that have been prescribed as necessary for employment.

In this particular context the course framework had been adapted to offer a part-time access route for bilingual students seeking entry to the college's BTEC National course (considered equivalent to 'A' level). There was a focus on developing students' Use of English, through double staffing, routine redrafting and resubmission of written work, reduced 'information input', and a maximum class size of 12. The approach to business studies was essentially 'investigative' including, for example, an exploration of local job opportunities and requirements, a viability study of setting up a small business, and a report on the student's own community in the UK and business and trade links with their country of origin.

The course was seen as an important development in catering for the many students who want to study for a vocation in business, and who have become frustrated with 'general ESL classes' while still being denied entry to the mainstream BTEC courses by the entry tests in English Language. The class was exclusively for bilingual students, with the intention of students integrating into the mainstream BTEC National courses in subsequent years.

The student writers

Table 1

Name	Age	Sex	Country of origin	Language they used most in the home
Nazrul	17	M	UK/Bangladesh	Bengali
Syed	17	M	UK/Bangladesh	Sylheti
Balogun	23	M	Nigeria	Yoruba
Ajayi	22	M	Nigeria	Yoruba
Hatem	23	M	Yeman	Arabic

For this paper I have selected five male students who chose to talk about the same three texts. The whole study involved eight students (6M, 2F) from a class 12 (8M, 4F) who felt they had time available to talk to me. (Names are changed for confidentiality.)

While the students were described as 'ESL' and 'Second Language' students, all had in fact been educated through the medium of English: two in Nigeria, one in the Yeman and two in the UK. Nazrul and Syed, having been educated in the UK, had also spent respectively two and three years of their recent education in Bangladesh. They had been born here, whereas Hatem and Ajayi were here specifically for their education, and Balogun had come recently and temporarily with his family. They all had the intention of living both in Britain and in their other country.

Reasons for talking about specific texts

In a pilot study I had tried to talk about texts and writing but it seemed difficult to find a 'common language' to do so. The extensive dialogues from which I quote below were possible because we talked about specific pieces of writing the students had written. By having these texts in front of us we could:

(1) generate issues to talk about that the students may not have thought about in general terms;
(2) talk with a greater level of detail about these;
(3) avoid the dangers of 'general' conversations about writing where students may have responded more in terms of what they thought I wanted to hear than what they had experienced and thought;
(4) explore their understanding and conception of the character of the texts through the examples of those they had attempted to write.

Such an approach recognises that writing is contextual (Barton, 1991, Faigley, 1986), and that it is important to ask not 'how do you write?' but 'how did you write this?'.

In an attempt to make the interviews useful also to the students (see Cameron, 1992) I suggested that the interviews could help them in discovering what they had learned about writing to take from this course to the next. I invited them in a letter to choose and bring 'two pieces of writing you have done, one which you were pleased with, and one which you were unhappy with, either because of the writing or the comments/grade you received'. This was very important because it gave the students a purpose for talking about texts. It also actually made possible the most productive questions. These were not:

how did you know what you were aiming to produce?

or

tell me about writing this

as I had anticipated and therefore planned, but rather

why did you choose to talk about this?
did you enjoy writing it?

and

were you worried by it?

The latter appeared to be less daunting and less leading, and managed to raise points that would have been difficult to raise by direct questions.

Giving students the choice of texts to discuss did, however, mean that they brought some which they had written up to eight months previously. But any potential information that may have been lost as a result seemed to be more than compensated for by the fact that the students attached such significance to the texts and the points they discussed. There was a sense in which the feeling of pride and/or the existence of problems still unresolved, made these texts, the experience of them, and the thinking about them still very much current in the students' minds. In this way, asking them to choose did of course bring to the fore problematic rather than representative experiences from the course.

The tasks and the texts

The writing tasks were 'imposed' (Ivanic & Moss, 1991) by the institution, 'factual', assessed (in terms of skills demonstrated), and written both in and out of class time. Below I outline the tasks, giving both what was written or explained to me by the tutor, and a description of it by one of the students. The latter is necessary in recognition that a lot more information about the task is likely to have been absorbed from discussion and sources besides the task sheet, and that the students' writing will reflect their own construction or reinterpretation of the task. These brief statements alone begin to suggest that Syed constructed the first task in terms of 'action', and that Nazrul and Ajayi made a rather encyclopaedic interpretation of the report task.

A description of a visit (discussed by Syed and Nazrul):

On the task sheet:[1]
Visit with [ ] on [date]. Produce a written account of this visit

As described by Syed:
the task is to visit the [   ] city (.) and find out the area / and the rush hour / and in this area what (   ) high street / those things /

A proposal for a report (discussed by Nazrul and Hatem):

> From the task sheet and tutor (my summary):
>> to write a proposal for the report [below] stating the information to be included, the sources of this, and the dates for completion of parts of it

> As described by Nazrul:
>> *that was proposal for report about mother country / the economic and social cultures / area and population of Bangladesh / its contents of what's going to be in this report /*

The report (discussed by Hatem, Syed, Balogun and Ajayi):

> From the task sheet and tutor (my summary):
>> to research and write about, firstly, the country and area of origin of their language group, and secondly, the locations and employment opportunities of this language group when outside the country of origin

> As described by Ajayi:
>> *this is a research report of my mother tongue Nigeria / in which we are asked to find the economic activities of the country / both here and abroad /*

A view of genre

I use Swales' (1990: 57–8) 'working definition' of genre as a 'class of communicative events, the members of which share some set of communicative purposes'. While communicative purpose is his 'privileged criterion' he says that this 'shapes' and 'constrains' choice of content and style, so that 'exemplars of a genre' viewed as 'prototypical' by the discourse community will 'Exhibit . . . similarity in terms of structure, style, content and intended audience'. I represent these five inter-related elements below.

Communicative purpose

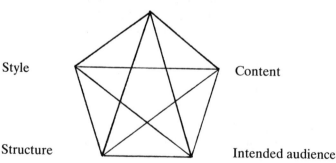

The findings below suggest that the students were engaging in decisions about these five elements of genre. I shall argue that they were therefore bringing implicit understandings of the generic characteristics of texts.

The Findings

In presenting this data it is difficult to capture both the individuals' descriptions of their texts as 'cases', revealing the ways in which they made sense of the texts in terms of their previous experience, and at the same time make the connections and similarities between individual accounts that reveal their shared patterns of experience. Within the limited space available here I shall focus on the shared themes that emerged and illustrate these from the comments of one or more individuals. I shall first identify issues about the students' perceived familiarity with the tasks and the types of texts required, and then attempt to capture some of their thinking about Swales' five elements of genre.

Perceived familiarity with the tasks and the types of text

Nazrul described two very different writing experiences. For his report proposal he *'didn't know how to do a (.) what to do / what part should go to where'*. In contrast for his description of the visit he says:

that wasn't worried me (.) . . . / because that was a bit easy / . . .

[at school] they will [would] ask me to do an incident or something / which I've written about the first day in my school in Bangladesh (   ) / and that one is similar /

Thus he explains why the task was *'a bit easy'* by constructing it as *'similar'* to his previous experience. Yet this similarity is not in terms of the content but apparently in terms of being *'an incident'* — the visit; his text is a chronologically structured description of personal action and observation.

This perception of familiarity with the task and the text appears to prompt a whole unproblematic writing process with which he is familiar and confident, summarised as *'first information / then roughly / once / then this one / the neat one'*. This contrasts with his writing process for the unfamiliar report proposal, where he describes more drafts, and uncertainty and changes of mind on quantity and structure.

Syed similarly describes an apparent ease with writing about the visit, and contrasts this with writing his report about Bangladesh. However, he conceptualises and explains this difference in terms of the nature of the language he perceives as required by the two tasks. Explaining his opening sentence about the visit 'I went to [   ] Street by bus and got off near [   ] Road', he says:

> *this is just the normal way of saying it / . . . / in a business way you can say (.) 'I have visited [   ] Road and I have seen there are lots of people in the high street (.) (   ) lots of things that can be found' / [here] I just using my own expression to describe the places*

His examples of his two alternative forms concur with Halliday's (1989b) description of 'spoken' forms of English (*'the normal way'*, *'my own expression'*) as more grammatically intricate, and written texts (*'a business way'*, *'plain English'*) as more lexically dense. Yet Syed's decision to adopt the *'normal way'* also has implications beyond the style or language of his text: his alternative forms would each lead to a different content focus (his personal action in visiting as opposed to the various features of the city centre); a different structure (chronological as opposed to thematic); and therefore a different communicative purpose (to describe his personal actions and perceptions as opposed to describing the city itself).

Interestingly neither Syed nor Nazrul received a high assessment from the tutor for this task, suggesting that the lecturer might have implicitly anticipated *'the business way'* and/or valued this kind of text more highly. For Syed at least the text he produced does not fairly represent his skills or ability to produce a description of the city, suggesting that a skills assessment that does not take into account his construction of the task and decisions in writing cannot adequately recognise his capability.

Like Nazrul, Syed identifies a difference in his writing strategies between the two tasks, explaining these in terms of his familiarity with his two forms of English. He prefers writing *'in the normal way'* because *'I know what I am writing about'*. Writing in *'plain English'* (*'the business way'*) apparently requires a more complex strategy which involves noting down the ideas and information as they come to mind, and then carrying out some kind of reformulation process:

> *I have to think about it and how to say it in plain English / and while I'm going to say it I might lose the words I've said before / unless I took a note down*

These students' writing strategies appear to support the argument by Barton (1991) that writing processes are better considered in terms of 'practices' which are related to particular contexts and types of texts. The implication is that writing experience, confidence and proficiency are therefore not singular, but multiple and varying between texts and contexts.

Decisions about aspects of the genre of the text

So far I have suggested that these students constructed the tasks, the texts and the writing practices in terms of specific previous experience of tasks they perceived as similar, and/or in terms of more general notions about texts. In doing so they made decisions about the purpose, style, structure, and content of the texts — decisions that determined the nature of their final text.

It is in terms of the students' decisions about genre that I will structure the remainder of this account. I will address their decisions about each element of Swales' definition of genre in turn. However, it will be clear that as with Syed's characterisation of the two forms of language, each kind of decision has implications for the other elements of the text genre, and that all relate to implicit or explicit decisions about communicative purpose.

Decisions about style and communicative purpose

Hatem read some examples from his report where on reflection he would change the style from his first draft; he characterises the change below in terms of the situation and audience of his text:

Yemen is situated on the left corner of the Middle East' / . . . / you would never write something like this and let other people read it (.) especially for an exhibition / I mean you crack up from laughing (.) because 'on the left corner' — you're not playing football are you! / . . . it's true / I mean I'm just commenting on something I wrote and I know my mistake /

When I asked him what he will change it to, he was able to formulate an alternative wording that would be generally accepted as more appropriate to his report text:

. . . errr . . . I would say 'Yemen is situated (.) in the Middle East (.) from the north Saudi (.) from the east Oman' something like that

He also describes his difficulty in writing the *'opening sentence'* of the report, expressing dissatisfaction with the phrases that immediately came to mind, and explaining his practice of *'going sometimes to a book / and see how they open it'* because:

this writing is like writing a story — 'the reason I am writing to you is because' [he laughs] / it's easy to do that but you want to do it another way /

He tells me how he chose his opening phrase 'From the dawn of history the Yemani's established a great civilisation'. In doing so he reveals an appreciation of a 'discourse of history', and of what Swales describes almost as the PR role of the introduction of a text:

> *I did it like this / I saw the publishing for the Yemani things / . . . I wouldn't have started like this (.) myself / but it sounds — it goes with the rhythm like music / it just sounds (.) better / it's history so you make it sound as (.) as history / you make it interesting for the reader (.) this way / from the opening I think*

Clearly, from his knowledge of texts he is able to perceive and explain the need for such a style in his opening. Because this is not already confidently within his own writing repertoire, he achieves it through researching published texts. In this way he brings different practices into his writing in this section of the text.

This practice suggests there is perhaps an undefinable line between drawing on the language and style of published texts and what might be criticised by the teacher as 'copying'. Balogun, in expressing dismay at the allegation of 'copying' in his section on the geology of Nigeria, explains that he was unable to reformulate it because he did not know enough about the content. In his case he decided to include it because a report is *'not something you can do sat on your own . . . / you have to get information elsewhere . . . / so that's why you just have to quote'*. Both Hatem and Balogun therefore identify as conscious decisions their inclusion in their text of the words of others, and in explaining these decisions reveal considerable understanding about the generic character and communicative purpose of the text or section. The accusation of copying seems to fail to recognise these decisions and the rationale for 'importing' the text. It also prevents the students discovering the proximity of their practices to experienced writers' practices of quoting and drawing on recognisable discourse.

Balogun and Ajayi also explain that even the written style of 'their own writing' in their reports is actually different from that in their other more office-based tasks on the course. Balogun explains that he is *'familiar with — you know — when it comes to writing anything about government . . . / I can already do that on my own'*.

Like Nazrul, they both describe bringing to the task familiar writing practices from their past experience, as a result of perceiving familiarity with the task or the text — but in this case describing the familiarity in terms of content. However, they too are not 'successful' in the task, apparently failing to realise that their familiar skills and practices (they describe reproducing 'facts' for an exam) are not so highly valued in continuously assessed course work in this different cultural context.

Decisions about structure and communicative purpose

In parallel to Hatem (researching published texts for the style of his introduction) Balogun described researching the structure for his report by looking at some reports in the public library.

> *in the library I have take the time just to — I looked at some — you know — some of the reports people have made / so . . . that's what I have in mind with that / . . . I've got my contents / I've got the sources of informa- tion / I've got everything that — you know — that you have if you have to make a report*

In this way these students appear to have been engaged in a kind of 'un- official' genre analysis, basing their decisions about their own text on what they find in published texts they perceive as similar. For Balogun this appears unsuccessful, as his report is criticised for having the pictures and graphs at the back rather than throughout the text. He explains why he put them there in terms of his library research:

> *most of the reports I checked were not dealing with pictures . . . / if I had seen that I could have seen how I should have done it / . . . / they just had pictures at the back / and they call it — you know — appen- dices /*

His genre research and his decisions had not been discussed, and this seemed at least partly the result of a fear of this being evidence of his 'copy- ing'. But he was left feeling he didn't know what a report *'should look like'*, and assuming a single correct format existed that he had not achieved; an opportunity for a potentially informative discussion relating the structure and purpose of different reports had been lost.

Decisions about content and communicative purpose

As suggested by Nazrul and Ajayi's descriptions of the report (above) they appeared to construct it as an encyclopedic document, while somehow also recognising the impossibility of such a task:

Balogun: *what matters is . . . what you've got to present / and from the way I did mine . . . I cover everything on Nigeria*

Ajayi: *I was worried about it / because it's a (.) very large . . . big country (.) for you to cover all everything (.) of Nigeria*

Here in the absence of discussion to establish the generic identity and communicative purpose of their text, they appear to bring a communicative purpose of impressing the tutor with sheer quantity of information. This is seemingly supported by drawing on the encyclopaedia as a source text without appreciating its different identity; like an encyclopaedia, parts of their texts provide large quantities of categorical information devoid of explicit sources.

Decisions about intended audience and communicative purpose

When asked about the audience/reader of their text all students gave a rather 'blank' response, sometimes followed by the name of the tutor. However, it was when asking about their sense of enjoyment in writing that references to other audiences emerged.

Me: *what did you enjoy about it? /*

Ajayi: *it's really in the sense that I was able to give (.) what can be found —
or what (.) my country look like to other people / which is unknown
to them / so that they can read it and know what is going on in other
countries /*

Ajayi explains this purpose in terms of importance of knowing about other countries to *'adjust to'* the people, and, in this case, in terms of encouraging people to visit Nigeria. Syed and Hatem also reveal similar aims, identifying their audience as British people who would say *'where is Yeman?'* or who believe *'false facts'* about Bangladesh. Like Balogun and Ajayi their purpose was to communicate a positive image of their country. This may have been the rationale for the personal introductions to the reports, introducing themselves and their cultural group, and Ajayi's expressed intention to make his text *'simple and straightforward'*.

This aim to communicate something that mattered to them seemed to be at the root of their distress with the skills assessment. In the terminology of Johns & Davies (1983), for the students their text had become a 'vehicle for information', but the lecturer responded to it as a 'language object' focusing on the language skills apparently revealed by the text, as if the information itself was of no importance.

Their communicative purpose and intended audience appeared as the rationale behind their selection of information content in at least parts of their texts. Yet because they were not made explicit or shared with the lecturer they led to a mismatch between his and their judgements about what kinds of information and levels of detail should be included. In the assessment the lecturer criticises these aspects and the students' 'selection skills'. Again the criticism of skills seems inappropriate without knowing the students' communicative purpose in their writing. With a greater understanding of the students' construction of the task, the teacher could have either assessed their skills in achieving it, or redirected their intentions. Either way, the implications of audience and purpose could be discussed and then applied more consistently through the text; the students could also learn how to make these explicit in the introduction to their text.

Conclusions and Pedagogical Implications

My first question was how do these students conceive and manage to meet the genre-specific demands on their texts. It would appear that in order to conceptualise the texts they are aiming to produce, the students made associations with other tasks and texts in their past experience, and, on the basis of this perceived familiarity, made decisions about the nature of their current text.

The students appeared to make decisions about some or all of Swales' elements of genre. Moreover, when they perceived aspects of the genre as new and unfamiliar to them, they endeavoured to explore published texts they perceived as similar, engaging in a kind of solitary, unacknowledged and undeveloped form of genre analysis.

The students seemed to closely associate familiar texts with familiar writing practices, which they then brought to the task at hand. For different genres of texts, and for texts perceived as familiar and unfamiliar, they appeared to adopt different writing strategies, sometimes experimental and exploratory and sometimes based on their experiences with previous writing tasks.

The students' understanding of the language and character of different texts, their decisions about these, their investigations into less familiar aspects of the genre, and their uses of known or new writing strategies, were not transparent in their texts. They were therefore not recognised nor affirmed or disaffirmed by the feedback and assessment. The assessments suggest that it is problematic to assume that the skills and understandings involved in producing a text can be adequately inferred from the final product. Murray's observation that 'process cannot be inferred from product any more than a pig can be inferred from a sausage' (Murray, 1982: 18) appeared particularly apt!

My second question was whether a pedagogy based on reflection on students' own competence was feasible with these students. There would certainly appear to be a rich foundation for such an approach. The students appeared sophisticated in their thinking about language and texts in English despite being rejected by the mainstream course entry tests in English.

When talking about specific texts that they had been so involved in, they could discuss their understandings and decisions, and both reveal and develop their explicit KAL.

The students were also very keen to talk about their texts, apparently because these mattered in terms of the assessment and in terms of what they had set out to do. In some cases this was prompted by a pride in their writing, and in others by unresolved questions that they wanted to discuss. Indeed because the assessment did not recognise or inform their decisions during writing, there was a considerable *need* to talk. This actually suggests a need for a writing pedagogy based on reflection on competence, since without it so much of the potential learning from the tasks seems to have been missed. It also suggests that the relative focus on form vs. content in teacher-feedback (Fatham & Whalley, 1990) may be less important than engaging with the actual decisions students are making.

Interestingly, the need to discuss and inform the students' decisions was often greatest in the apparently least difficult texts. Because their previous educational experience had been within a different cultural context, students' perceptions of familiarity with the task frequently led to an 'unsuccessful' text, as their perceptions did not match with the (implicit) expectations and demands of their UK lecturers.

For the teacher to be able to recognise and inform the decisions students are taking would require considerable communication *from* the student *to* the teacher during the writing process. For this reason, the process of guiding students' reflection on their texts and writing practices would appear to be important in informing the teacher as well as the student. For both it would bring to explicit discussion and awareness the complex language issues that students are actually dealing with — and/or would find it most useful to address — in their writing.

Note

1. [   ] indicates text deleted for confidentially.
   [below] indicates text added by me to assist the reader.
   (   ) indicates inaudible utterances in the interview.
   (.) indicates a pause.

References

Barton, D. (1991) The social nature of writing. In D. Barton and R. Ivanic (eds) Writing in the community. *Written Communication Annual: An International Survey of Research and Theory* Vol. 6, 1–13. California: Sage Publications Inc.
Bourne, J. (1989) *Moving into the Mainstream: LEA Provision for Bilingual Pupils.* UK: NFER-Nelson.

Cameron, D. (1992) 'Respect, please!': Investigating race, Power and language. In D. Cameron, E. Frazer, P. Harvey, M. B. H. Rampton and K. Richardson *Researching Language: Issues of Power and Method*. London: Routledge.

Carter, R. (ed.) (1990) *Knowledge about Language and the Curriculum: The LINC Reader*. London: Hodder & Stoughton.

Faigley, L. (1986) Competing theories of process: A critique and a proposal. In *College English* 48, 6, 527–42.

Fatham, A. K. and Fatham, E. W. (1990) Teacher response to student writing: Focus on form versus content. In B. Kroll (ed.) *Second Language Writing: Research Insights from the Classroom*. Cambridge University Press.

Halliday, M. (1989a) Part A of M. Halliday and R. Hasan *Language, Context, and Text: Aspects of Language in a Social-Semiotic Perspective*. Oxford University Press.

— (1989b) *Spoken and Written language*. Oxford University Press.

Ivanic, R. and Moss, W. (1991) Bringing community writing practices into Education. In D. Barton and R. Ivanic (eds) Writing in the community. *Written Communication Annual: An International Survey of Research and Theory* Vol. 6, 1–13. California: Sage Publications Inc.

Johns, T. and Davies, F. (1983) Text as a vehicle for information: The classroom use of written texts in teaching reading in a foreign language. *Reading in a Foreign Language* 1, 1, 1–19.

Murray, D. (1982) *Learning by Teaching*. Montclair, New Jersey: Boynton/Cook.

Raimes, A. (1987) Language proficiency, writing ability, and composing strategies: A study of ESL college student writers. *Language Learning* Vol. 37, no. 3, 439–68.

Swales, J. M. (1990) *Genre Analysis: English in Academic and Research Settings*. Cambridge University Press.

5 Japanese College Students' Attitudes Towards Non-native Varieties of English

HIROKO MATSUURA, *Kaetsu Womens' Junior College*
REIKO CHIBA, *Asia University*
ASAKO YAMAMOTO, *Nihon University*

Introduction

The spread of English as a world language has been given considerable attention by sociolinguists for at least the last 10 years. Kachru (1989) estimated total users of English around the world to be 750 million, among whom 350 million are native speakers of English and 400 million are non-native speakers. English is the principal means of intercommunication not only among native speakers but also between native speakers and non-native speakers, and between non-native speakers and non-native speakers.

Linguistically, Japan can be categorised as an EFL country, where English is learned as a mandatory subject but is not used outside of class. The English-speaking population is very small and nearly 100% Japanese use the Japanese language at home. However, with Japan's economic and technological progress, more and more Japanese have been exposed to different varieties of English in their work-settings or when travelling abroad. Regrettably, it seems that in many places non-native English is not always perceived positively by the Japanese.

Language attitude is not a new field of inquiry. More than 30 years ago, Lambert *et al.* (1960) investigated attitudes to spoken language by analysing the evaluative reactions of both English and French speakers in Canada toward English and French. Lambert *et al.* developed a *matched guise* technique, which involved the same individual (bilingual) reading a passage in different language varieties and letting the subjects listen to the passage and react by choosing adjectives from a chart. The subjects were not aware that the same individual was used to read everything, and therefore, the evaluational reactions to the two language guises could be matched for each speaker.

While the matched guise technique was essential to elicit attitudes towards speakers, the semantic differential technique used by Osgood (1964) provided a good framework for developing an evaluation chart. The semantic differential used a list of opposite adjective pairs arrayed by bi-polar rating scales. The subjects indicated their reactions on the chart by choosing a number from one to seven. Osgood suggested that adjectives in the scale were grouped into two factors: *Evaluation* (e.g. good–bad, pleasant–unpleasant, positive–negative), and *Potency* (e.g. fast–slow, active–passive, excitable–calm).

In the field of language learning and teaching research, there have been a number of attitudinal studies using techniques which follow Lambert & Osgood. Carranza & Ryan (1975) examined evaluative reactions of Mexican-American and Anglo high school students toward speakers of standard English and standard Spanish. The results indicated that Spanish was rated higher in the home context, and English, on the other hand, was rated higher in the school context. Oller, Hudson & Liu (1977) conducted a study on the effect of Chinese students' attitudes on proficiency in ESL. Generally, students who were more integratively motivated performed better than those who were less integratively motivated. Similarly, in Hong Kong, Pierson, Fu & Lee (1982) analysed the relationship between English language attainment and attitudes toward English among Chinese-speaking secondary school students. The statistical results indicated that the direct measure (e.g. to pass school entrance exams, to see the United States, and to get to know Americans) of attitude was a better predictor of English attainment than an indirect measure (stereotyped adjectives). In France, Flaitz (1988) investigated French attitudes toward Anglo-American ideology, culture, people, and language. This elaborate research produced a number of interesting findings. For example, the subjects in the study perceived American English as a loud, fast direct language, while British English was seen as more elegant, rich, and slow; the United States was seen to function as the source of English as an international *lingua franca* in France; and there was no relationship found between subjects' proficiency and attitudes.

Although language attitude is not a new field of study we have not seen many attitude studies involving non-native varieties of English. The research we shall discuss below is particularly concerned with Japanese students' attitudes towards spoken non-native varieties of English.

The hypotheses addressed in the study are:

(1) The subjects will view American English more positively than other varieties of English.
(2) Positive and negative attitudes will not correlate significantly with proficiency in English.
(3) Motivational factors will contribute to the subjects' attitudes towards non-native accents.
(4) Subjects who perceive English as a world language will be more tolerant of non-native accents.

Method

Subjects

The experiments were conducted at two different universities. Fifty-three of the 92 subjects were majoring in English, and the other 39 subjects were majoring in international business. Most of the subjects received six years of English education in junior and senior high school as one of their school subjects, with the exception of 17 subjects who lived in foreign countries for more than one year. Six years is the typical length of English study prior to college.

Speakers

Recording was done by seven speakers. Six speakers were international students at Asia University in Tokyo (Malay, Chinese Malay, Bangladeshi, Micronesian, Hong Kongese, Sri Lankan). These countries were chosen because English is spoken as a second language in those places (Platt, Weber & Ho, 1984).

One speaker was an American instructor at Asia University. The American speaker was included to elicit differential attitudes toward non-native and native varieties from the subjects. All speakers were male. The six student speakers were asked to provide information about their English education and the use of English in their countries.

Materials

The paragraph

The paragraph which the speakers read was chosen from an ESL textbook. It consisted of 79 words and described an incident of former Japanese Prime Minister Noboru Takeshita.

Questionnaire A

Ten sets of adjectives arrange in bi-polar rating scales were used to elicit the subjects' impression of each speaker's English. To avoid a left-right bias, half the scales had positive adjectives on the left and half the positive on the right, though during statistical analyses the points were adjusted so that the highest point was seven and the lowest was one.

Questionnaire B

The subjects were asked to answer a questionnaire on their ideas about foreign languages and countries using a seven-point rating scale (1 = completely agree — 7 = completely disagree).

The questionnaire consisted of 16 statements such as 'I study English because it is required for graduation' (shown in Table 2), and four questions: 'Do you have friends or acquaintances in foreign countries? If yes, in which countries?; Have you lived abroad? If yes, where, when and how long?; What languages do you want to be able to speak?; What countries are you interested in?'

CELT

This standardised test is often used to determine learners' proficiency in English. It consists of three parts — listening, vocabulary, and grammar. In this study, the subjects' scores on CELT were used to examine the relation between English proficiency and attitudes toward non-native accents of English.

Procedures

The subjects were asked to listen to the tape and indicate their impression of each speaker using the sets of adjectives (Questionnaire A). The tape recorder was stopped after each speaker was heard so that the subjects could rate each speaker individually. When all speakers had been heard, the experimenters announced the end of the experiment.

The subjects were also asked to answer Questionnaire B on their ideas about foreign languages and countries. On a different day, the CELT was conducted during class hours. The subjects were told that the test results would not be considered for their grades, but just for general information concerning their English proficiency.

Results and Discussion

Overall, the subjects showed more positive reactions toward the American accent than they did toward the non-native accents in this research. Scores

Table 1 Means and SDs of the scores for N and NN accent (N = 92)

Variables	Non-native		Native	
	Mean	*SD*	*Mean*	*SD*
X1	3.68	1.49	5.26	1.41
X2	2.58	1.40	5.25	1.48
X3	3.30	1.41	5.12	1.66
X4	3.75	1.41	4.57	1.61
X5	3.40	1.18	4.77	1.22
X6	3.61	1.20	5.43	1.06
X7	3.14	1.43	5.25	1.93
X8	3.79	1.03	4.88	1.14
X9	2.95	1.32	5.35	1.28
X10	3.90	1.27	4.42	1.27
T1	34.07	7.20	50.31	7.47

that the subjects gave to each accent variety in Questionnaire A were summed, and the respective mean scores to the native and the non-native were calculated. Table 1 indicates the Mean and SD of the scores for the native accent and non-native accent group. Figure 1 shows the profile of the impression for these accent variables. This profile implies that the subjects might have been able to differentiate the native accent from the other varieties.

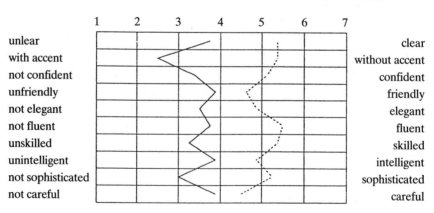

Note: \ = non-native accents; ⋱ = native accents

Figure 1 Profile of ratings given to non-native and native accents

Earlier, we listed some hypotheses in terms of the subjects' attitudes toward the native and non-native accents. We will try to validate those hypotheses.

The American speaker received more positive reactions than did the rest of the speakers. This finding was extracted from the results of a t-test for matched groups. The mean score for the native accent was significantly greater than the mean for the non-native accents ($t = 15.53, p < 0.001$). This is probably because many subjects were relatively familiar with North American English, and therefore they gave favourable ratings to the American accent.

Subjects who collaborated in this research had at least six years of English education in Japan — three years at junior high school and three years at high school. Generally, instructional models at those schools feature North American English with the exception of the occasional British or Australian English model. Even if a Japanese teaches an English class using his/her native language, students are exposed to the target American English by means of audiotapes and some other materials. It can be assumed that most subjects in this research easily guessed that one of the speakers was actually American and that many of the subjects had a preference for North American English. On one of the questionnaires, 43 subjects stated that they had friends or acquaintances either in the United States or Canada. However, many subjects might have felt the non-native varieties less favourable because of their unfamiliarity with them.

Our second hypothesis was that positive and negative attitudes would not correlate with English Proficiency. Pearson Correlation Coefficients were used to validate this hypothesis. We assumed that a subject's attitudes toward the English varieties could be observed in the difference between his/her total score for the native speaker and the total score for the non-native speakers (N–NN). That is a large N–NN differential meant the impression for spoken native and non-native English was more different. The Pearson Correlation Coefficient between CELT and N–NN indicated that subjects' attitudes toward native and non-native did not correlate with English proficiency at a significant level. This point confirms the view of Cooper & Fishman (1977, 263–4), in their investigation of Israeli students' achievement and attitudes, who stated that 'respondents' views of Americans, favourable or unfavourable, made little difference with respect to English achievement or usage', and that much the same could be said about the English language.

Factor analyses and correlation analyses were employed with respect to testing our third and fourth hypotheses, which were 'Motivational factors will contribute to the subjects' attitudes toward non-native accents', and 'Subjects who perceive English as a world language will be more tolerant of non-native accents'. First, factor analyses were conducted to determine the dimension underlying the ratings given for Questionnaire B (16 items) by the subjects. The resulting 16*16 correlation matrix was subject to a principal factor analysis using an eigenvalue greater than 1.0 as criterion for extraction. The extracted factors were then rotated according to the varimax principle. The results of the rotation indicate that six factors underlie the scales employed in Questionnaire B and these account for 67% of the total variance. The items with factor loading greater than 0.4 were employed for the factor interpretation (Table 2). The mean and SD of each factor are also shown in Table 2. To reveal the relationships between the N–NN scores in Questionnaire A and each factor, correlation coefficients were calculated (Table 3).

Subjects who agreed to the items in Factor 4 — subjects with preference for American and British English — tended to show positive reactions when they heard the American accent, and, in turn, they gave relatively negative reactions to the non-native accents. This tendency was observed in the weak negative correlation found between the item mean of Factor 4 and N–NN. Generally speaking, the more positive the students were toward American and British English, the more positive they were likely to be toward the American accent they heard. The subjects' general preference for American and British English probably affected what they really chose as a better sounding accent. This is quite natural if a subject who likes American pronunciation could guess that one of the speakers was American or if s/he at least speculated that one of the accents s/he had heard was closest to an American accent.

There was a weak positive correlation between Factor 5 and N–NN. There is only one item representing Factor 5, which is 'I study English because it is required for graduation'. The idea might relate to an instrumental motivation in learning English. It can be said that a subject with less instrumental motivation was likely to be more positive toward the native accent and more negative toward the non-native accents. In other words, subjects who do not think they study English merely in order to graduate tended to have a bigger discrepancy in their attitudes toward the native and non-native accents. On the other hand, students who are more instrumentally motivated seem to react to non-native accents in the same manner as they do to native accents. But this is a hypothetical view and further research needs to be conducted to validate it.

A weak positive correlation was seen between Factor 6 and N–NN. This implies that subjects who agreed with the idea of Factor 6 tended to have little

Table 2 Factor analysis of questionnaire B with means and SDs for each factor

		FL	*Mean*	*SD*
Factor 1: Desire to learn and use English for practical and personal purposes				
5)	I want to talk to American or British people using English.	0.62	1.79	1.18
8)	I am willing to respond if spoken to in English.	0.57	2.41	1.42
2)	I want to learn English because I want to be educated.	0.56	2.81	1.53
13)	I want to learn about the cultures of the USA, UK and Canada.	0.46	2.67	1.49
3)	English is more useful in job hunting than other foreign languages.	0.43	2.78	1.44
14)	I want to talk to Asian people using English.	0.43	3.24	1.60
Factor 2: Englishism in language				
9)	English should be used as an international *lingua franca*.	0.70	3.42	1.56
10)	Education in Japan should be done in English.	0.61	6.14	1.14
Factor 3: Ethnocentricism in language				
11)	Foreigners should speak Japanese when they are in Japan.	0.85	3.69	1.75
12)	When in a foreign country, people should speak the language of that country.	0.56	2.70	1.50
Factor 4: Preference for American and/or British English				
16)	I want to learn American English rather than Australian or Singaporean English.	0.69	2.59	1.56
7)	I want to pronounce English as American or British people do.	0.49	1.63	1.09
4)	I like the sounds of English.	0.46	2.36	1.49
Factor 5: Instrumental motivation in learning English				
1)	I study English because it is required for graduation.	0.69	5.94	1.37
Factor 6: Nativism in language				
15)	In any country, the native language should be most respected.	0.71	1.70	1.32

Table 3 Pearson correlation coefficients between factors and N–NN

	Correlation coefficients	
	r	p
Factor 1	−0.11403	0.2873
Factor 2	−0.08495	0.4287
Factor 3	−0.01321	0.9022
Factor 4	−0.22584	0.0333
Factor 5	0.28194	0.0074
Factor 6	0.21870	0.0395

difference between their attitudes toward the native accent and attitudes toward the non-native accents. The idea representing Factor 6 was that '[i]n any country, the native language should be most respected'. It appeared that subjects agreeing with this had a propensity to show no or fewer negative feelings toward indigenous varieties of languages. Most probably, non-native English accents were perceived by many subjects in the same way as they might perceive indigenous varieties of languages. They tended to perceive accents of native speakers in the same positive way as they perceived those of non-native speakers.

The results of correlation studies imply that the third and fourth hypotheses are true to some extent. Especially, the correlation analysis between Factor 6 and the subjects' attitudes toward spoken non-native English indicates that people respecting indigenous languages seem to be more tolerant of non-native accents. We believe that respecting indigenous varieties of English is most desirable in the context of English as a world language. As an Indian linguist, Kachru (1985, 1987, 1989), has always noted, English is not only for native speakers of English but also for non-native speakers. We hope that all Japanese will view non-native Englishes in the same positive manner as they view American and British English.

Conclusion

The subjects evaluated the native accent more positively than the non-native accents, as we hypothesised. It is assumed that this differential attitude is grounded on the fact that a North American variety is often heard as a model in Japanese classroom settings. Another finding is that the subjects'

English proficiency did not significantly correlate with the difference in attitudes toward native and non-native accents. Thus, the second hypothesis was also proved. Furthermore, the subjects who were assumed to study English with instrumental motivation tended not to differentiate their attitudes toward native and non-native accents, though this was only weakly indicated. In addition, the subjects who respected a native language in any country also showed similar attitudes toward native and non-native accents. Hypotheses 3 and 4 were, therefore, indirectly proved.

A number of issues remain to be examined in future studies. First, motivational factors were not clearly extracted due to the limitation of Questionnaire B. Second, the perception of world Englishes needs to be defined so that the relation between attitudes and perception can be identified.

References

Carranza, M. A. and Ryan, E. B. (1975) Evaluative reactions of bilingual Anglo and Mexican American adolescents toward speakers of English and Spanish. In *International Journal of the Sociology of Language* 6, 83–104.

Cooper, R. L and Fishman, J. A. (1977) A study of language attitudes. In J. A. Fishman, R. L. Coooper and A. W. Conrad (eds) *The Spread of English*. Rowley, MA: Newbury House.

Flaitz, J. (1988) *The Idiology of English: French Perceptions of English as a World Language*. Berlin: Mouton de Gruyter.

Kachru, B. B. (1985) Institutionalized second-language varieties. In S. Greenbaum (ed.) *The English Language Today*. Oxford: Pergamon Press.

— (1987) The spread of English and sacred linguistic cows. In P. Lowenberg (ed.) *Language Spread and Language Policy: Issues, Implications, and Case Studies*. Washington, DC: Georgetown University Press.

— (1989) Teaching World Englishes. In *Indian Journal of Applied Linguistics 15*, 85–95.

Lambert, W. E., Hodgson, C., Gardner, C. and Fillenbaun, S. (1960) Evaluative reactions to spoken languages. In *Journal of Abnormal and Social Psychology* 60, 44–51.

Oller, J. W., Hudson, A. J. and Liu, P. F. (1977) Attitudes and attained proficiency in ESL: A sociolinguistic study of native speakers of Chinese in the United States. In *Language Learning* 27, 1–27.

Osgood, C. E. (1964) Semantic differential technique in the comparative study of cultures. In *American Anthropologist* 66 (3), Part 2, 171–200.

Pierson, H.D., Fu, G. S.and Lee, S. (1982) An analysis of the relationship between language attitudes and English attainment of secondary students in Hong Kong. In *Language Learning* 30, 289–316.

Platt, J. H., Weber, H. and Ho, M. L. (1984) *The New Englishes*. London: Routledge.

6 Evaluating Computer Assisted Language Learning from the Learners' Point of View

PHIL SCHOLFIELD, *University of Wales Bangor*
GEORGE YPSILADIS, *Aristotle University of Thessaloniki*

Introduction: CALL and Theory

The relationship between Computer Assisted Language Learning (CALL) and general approaches to language learning and teaching has evolved considerably over the years. In the early days when computers filled a whole room and projects like PLATO got underway in America, CALL might be described as having been very much theory-*driven*. The theory that did the driving in those behaviorist days, and, for some, continues to do so today, was that of 'programmed learning'. Learners sat before the machine learning Russian through a series of drills and tests which either sent them on to the next step or back to do more work on the last. Though programmed learning materials can, and were, produced in book form, the computer by nature seemed eminently suited to this approach. For a mechanical method of language teaching what better than a machine to deliver it?

Nowadays research has considerably changed our views about how languages are learnt. Correspondingly many practitioners' ideas about what is pedagogically appropriate in language teaching have changed radically. Amongst other things we have witnessed the rise to favour of 'communicative language teaching', and the emphasis on 'learner-centredness'. More recently 'language awareness' has come to the fore as an important notion. Concurrently the nature and availability of computers has changed almost out of recognition, though in many ways what computers can actually *do* — the 'software' — has not changed so much.

In this climate CALL has become what one might describe as 'theory-*accommodated*'. Rather than abandoning the computer as, for the time being at least, unsuited to modern pedagogical ideas, some people have used considerable ingenuity to find ways in which it can be used compatibly with communicative language teaching (e.g. Jones & Fortescue, 1987), or to enhance a language awareness program (e.g. Scholfield, 1991), and so forth. In the process, the emphasis has shifted somewhat from the computer programs *per se* to the way they are used, since often a program that in itself appears to have little pedagogical value can be totally transformed by the activity it is embedded in. For instance an adventure game that appears linguistically to entail only a little reading comprehension of instructions on-screen, if made the focus of group interaction off-screen discussing what choices to make, can involve a tremendous amount of genuine oral communication. A list of models or roles for the computer in language learning additional to the obvious and original one of tutor or surrogate teacher has emerged — the computer as stimulus (e.g. adventure games), as reference resource (e.g. databases, concordances, hypertext materials), as workhorse/ instrument (e.g. word-processing), and even as tutee (where the learner 'teaches' the computer). See further Ng & Olivier, 1987; Phillips, 1987.

Something shared by CALL at all periods of its development is the enthusiasm it generates in its proponents. Programs are written and activities proposed largely by a relatively small number of people, not all of whom have much pedagogical experience, or familiarity with all the disciplines whose theories should inform CALL (e.g. Applied Linguistics, Psychology, Education, Computing). Books and articles tend to convey an optimistic tone that is not yet adequately supported by a great deal of *objective* evaluation, to which we now turn.

Evaluation of CALL

Like any pedagogical materials and activities, CALL, or a specific instance of CALL, potentially can be evaluated in terms both of its underlying theory and its actual execution in practice. On the theory side, since as we have seen many CALL activities with various programs can be shown to be compatible in principle with a number of standpoints on language learning and teaching, any critique of CALL will largely devolve into a critique of one or more of those standpoints, or involve arguing that CALL for some logical reason can or cannot actually be implemented in a way compatible with them. Evaluation of these sorts is of course a fundamental task, but too vast a matter to be pursued here.

CALL also can and should be evaluated by empirical study of its practical instantiation in classrooms and self-access rooms. Witness the dictum of Blondel *et al.* (1991) 'CALL should not be evaluated in isolation'. This is desirable for at least two reasons. First, where CALL programs and activities are being implemented in a way that one can assume definitely reflects some underlying philosophy of language learning or teaching, e.g. because a researcher has ensured this by experimental control, then evaluation of CALL in action is effectively another way of evaluating that underlying theory. Second, where, as in the minimally interventional study below, no such fixed relationship can be assumed, evaluation is rather of aspects of the implementation itself. Particular programs and activities are evaluated *per se*, and so indirectly are the programmers and teachers responsible for them. CALL in general does not stand or fall by this, but it remains vital for the guidance of day to day teaching to gather information with more modest evaluative goals. Three broad approaches to investigation are commonly used (cf. Hamburger, 1990), each with their strengths and weaknesses but hopefully together leading ultimately to a consensus on good practice.

(1) The teacher or researcher can rely on his/her personal introspection based on experience, using a checklist of evaluation points. These often cover a wide range of variables related to the technical ease and practical pedagogical usefulness of the programs; their linguistic content, and whether language improvement seems to occur when they are used; what users' attitudes seem to be, etc. This approach is really a formalisation of the 'I think this works/will work' level of discussion typical of a lot of the literature on CALL. It can lack objectivity unless the intuitions of more than one 'expert' are tapped, and judgments collected by someone other than the judge, in a proper survey. (See e.g. Akahori 1988; Ng & Olivier, 1987; Swartz *et al.*, 1990; Odell, 1986; Jones & Fortescue, 1987.)

(2) One can do 'classic' research on the effectiveness of CALL by comparing groups using CALL with groups not using it, over a period. There would be a pretest of various aspects of the learners' language ability, a treatment period, and a post-test to determine language achievement. This is usually done experimentally and for language ability only (which may be variously defined in terms of correctness or fluency, etc.), though attitudes and other variables could be included. There are well known problems with the elimination of unwanted factors and the lack of illumination of the processes by which outcomes are arrived at. (See e.g. Horton *et al.*, 1988 and studies reported in Ahmad *et al.*, 1985: 119ff.)

(3) One can do research more of the ethnographic type, observing quasi-naturalistically and/or eliciting learner self-reports and/or using records retained by the computer of each user's choices, errors, etc. This is

usually non-experimental and often focuses on many variables other than those of language performance, e.g. learner attitude, experience of the technical aspects of computer use, etc. (See e.g. Johnston, 1985; Windeatt, 1986; Poulsen, 1990; Blondel *et al.*, 1991; Kenning, 1991.)

The present study is of the third type, and is designed not only to add to our understanding of CALL in practice but also to demonstrate that this approach has more potential for rigour and detailed analysis than some studies of this sort so far conducted suggest. Studies hitherto have not usually compared the same programs being used in different ways, but have tended rather to compare one program with another or to compare activities with CALL programs with those without. Yet if CALL really is as much a matter of what you do with programs as what the programs do (Jones, 1986), this is a crucial variable to explore. Another difference from many previous studies is that neither were the learners new to CALL nor the programs new to the learners. Hence 'novelty' effect should not produce a misleadingly favourable result. Finally, unlike in many other studies, the researchers/ evaluators were not the teachers or programmers directly involved, so had no natural inclination to see things through rose-coloured glasses.

The study is largely exploratory, though differences between programs, modes of use, and age of learner were expected. In general, though well-established programs were being used in apparently uncontroversial ways, it was anticipated that all might not be as well in practice as it first might appear.

The Thessaloniki Study: Method

Subjects

The subjects were 48 Greek learners of English of intermediate level studying in Thessaloniki, Greece either in the British Council or a private language school. All had studied English for at least two years and used CALL in some form or other for at least two months, often a year at least, typically for one lesson per week. The age range was 12 to 37, with most subjects in the 15–25 band: the younger subjects were of course still at school, the older ones at university or adult learners.

Explanatory variables and design

Age was predicted as a potentially relevant variable from other studies (cf. Kenning & Kenning, 1990). Two further explanatory variables were incorporated — program and mode of use, each with three values. The three

programs were: Storyboard (WIDA Software), Screentest for First Certificate (Longman), and Gapmaster (WIDA Software). Storyboard is a text
reconstruction program which essentially presents text on screen with all the
letters of all the words replaced by squares. The immediate task is to restore
the text by asking to be given the minimum number of letters or words and
guessing correctly as many as possible. Gapmaster presents texts with gaps
for selected words. The task is to guess the missing words, with minimum use
of clues in the form of single letters. Screentest has a variety of sets of one-
sentence items with gaps to be filled or multiple choices to be selected from,
with no real help available. The items mostly focus on grammar or vocabulary
and are modelled on items in the Cambridge First Certificate Examination.

The three modes of use were as follows. 'Independent' use was where
subjects were using computers singly in a self-access room. 'Group' use was
where they were working in twos or threes round computers for 30 minutes
in a classroom with the teacher present, but not intervening unless asked.
'Class' use was where the teacher operated a single computer with screen
projected on a whiteboard and led the activity with the class as a whole for
60 minutes.

Ideally, with three programs and three modes of use one would have
studied nine groups covering all possible combinations. Since, however, it
had been decided to study CALL as naturalistically as possible in this
investigation, no intervention was made to create the ideal complete design.
Instead six groups were selected and studied as they were found actually
working in the normal way. They may be characterised as follows:

Program:	Storyboard		Screentest		Gapmaster	
Mode:	Group	Class	Indep.	Group	Group	Class
Place:	Brit C.	Priv.	Brit C.	Brit C.	Brit C.	Priv.
Age:	Older	Younger	Older	Older	Older	Younger

Dependent variables: Materials and procedure

Each subject was individually interviewed by one of the researchers
who went through a set of 28 questions in a non-threatening way, explaining
them in Greek where necessary. These questions all related to the learners'
experiences of and feelings about CALL as they were currently using it, and
were partly based on Odell's list for experts (1986) mentioned above. They
covered both technical and pedagogical variables, as will emerge in more
detail when the results are discussed below. Some were effectively questions
about what the learners did — *performance*, e.g. 'Do you find support
materials (dictionaries, notebooks, etc.) necessary when you use computers?'
Others were more about *attitude*, e.g. 'Would you prefer to work alone, in a

group, or with your teacher?' Others were more taxing, effectively requiring *meta*-judgments about language and the pedagogical process, such as one would normally elicit from teachers, e.g. 'Do you find the linguistic content suited to your language level?'.

In addition a researcher had previously observed one session of each of the six types involved, taking photographs and audio recording. This information proved invaluable in interpreting fully the questionnaire responses.

Results in Relation to the Explanatory Variables

Responses on 27 items were scored as ratings on either three or seven point scales. For ease of understanding in the account here they are all presented on a scale 0 to 6, with 0 indicating the most positive response and 6 the most negative. One further item was scored categorically.

Age

An examination of the results for marked correlations between age and responses on any of the questionnaire items revealed that age was largely irrelevant, perhaps a consequence of the fact that all subjects were quite accustomed to CALL. For instance there was negligible correlation between age and preference for computer-based learning ($r = -0.15$), though there was a slight but significant tendency for older subjects to find the program harder to load ($r = 0.3$). The most marked result was a correlation of 0.63 between age and claimed learning from off-screen interaction. That is, younger subjects claimed to learn more this way, but this may simply be a reflection of the fact that younger subjects were predominantly in the Class-mode groups which had interaction forced on them by the teacher. For related reasons perhaps, younger subjects claimed to need fewer support materials ($r = -0.42$).

Results not related to program or mode of use

We move now to group comparisons, for which the Kruskal-Wallis test was used and the .05 significance level adopted. As can be seen from Table 1, a considerable number of questions attracted responses that did not differ dependent on program or mode of use. The computer proved easy to use in all technical respects (A), as might be expected given that the programs were produced by quality software publishers and that the users had some prior experience of CALL. Attitudes to technical features (B) were also generally favourable. This all means that negative views of CALL that emerge on other variables below cannot simply be a consequence of difficulty with the technology.

Table 1 Matters on which there were no significant differences among the six groups

		Mean
TECHNICAL		
A	Ease of deleting letters	0.0
	Ease of getting help on screen	0.19
	Ease of quitting the program	0.38
	Ease of loading the program	0.5
	Ease of repeating the program	0.56
	Ease of moving the cursor	0.75
	Ease of understanding instructions	0.81
B	Helpfulness of colour	1.19
	Adequacy of number of options	0.21
PEDAGOGICAL		
C	Usefulness of words/text regardless of activity	0.81
	Usefulness of activity regardless of words/text	1.06
	Suitability of language to student level	1.31
	Suitability of program to student age	1.69
D	Suitability of program to personal needs	4.37
	Intrinsic interest of program	4.44
	Preference for computer-based learning	5.07
	Compatibility of program with other teaching	5.37
E	Adequacy of feedback provided by program	5.76

On a range of key pedagogical features of the programs and activities there was a marked division between four items that attracted reasonably favourable responses (C) and five that attracted unfavourable ones (D, E). The favourably judged features, it may be noted, are more 'objective' in nature. The users recognised that the CALL they were engaged in was suited to their age and level and involved things that were, in some detached sense, useful for learning English. However, they did not judge the programs suited to their own needs, which they mostly articulated as being real communication with English speakers. Nor did they regard the programs as fitting in with their other teaching, which was more communicative. It is not coincidental that they also found the programs uninteresting and would prefer non-CALL learning (see further the correlation analysis below).

Observation showed that indeed the activities were not implemented in a communication-oriented way, but were more medium-oriented and computer-focused; the teachers were not using the authoring facilities of Gapmaster and Storyboard to introduce variety of text and integrate the CALL with other teaching. We may also be seeing here the 'pall factor' at work — the reverse of the 'novelty factor' which may well have helped produce favourable results in other studies of CALL which did not use subjects with prior experience of the programs (e.g. Kenning, 1991).

The most negatively judged feature of all was the feedback provided by the computer. In fact Screentest gives the least feedback, simply telling users if they are right or not when they choose an answer, while Storyboard does the most, in the sense that users can ask for particular letters or words as clues to their guesses. However, none of these programs get near the limit of what is currently possible in feedback terms (which is still short of what a real teacher might provide of course). For instance the programs will not spot answers that are probably just mis-spellings of the right answer, or semantically close but not quite right; nor do they explain why one answer is better than another, or provide additional contextual clues and so on.

Programs

There were relatively few significant differences between programs (Table 2), and of course they have to be explained with an eye to the fact that program was not fully crossed with age or mode of use. In general it is Screentest that stands out from the other programs on a number of variables. A notable result was the rather more favourable view of Screentest's suitability to the learning task associated with it, which is matched by a slightly less negative view of its motivating effect, compared with the other two programs. This is readily explained not so much by the program *per se*

Table 2 Matters on which there were significant differences between programs

	Storyboard	Screentest	Gapmaster
Suitability of content to task	1.88	0.94	4.88
Motivating quality of computer task	6.0	4.31	5.25
Learning from off-screen interaction	2.82	5.82	2.63
Preference to work: Alone	38%	31%	25%
In group	56%	13%	44%
With teacher	6%	56%	31%

as by the fact that many of the users of Screentest were in fact preparing to take the Cambridge First Certificate Examination, to which the program is tailored, and had specifically *chosen* to use it. Hence they perceived a direct purpose for their CALL use while users of the other programs were using CALL as an adjunct to other teaching, with no very clearly defined purpose. Screentest also has a bit more variety of type of task within it, compared with the others which are both text-based cloze programs. The generally low level of claimed motivation is of course in marked contrast with the common claim made for CALL that it regularly inspires learners on tasks which they would not relish in pencil and paper form.

Since independent-mode CALL users were only using Screentest, it is not surprising that Screentest is associated with the least off-screen learning. The distinctive preference for Screentest users to work with the teacher may be associated with this last point, but may also reflect the fact that Screentest provides the least feedback within the program itself.

Modes of use

The first three differences between modes of use detailed in Table 3 all show distinctive results for the independent users, exclusively using Screentest. This may be for the same reasons just discussed, though these users' more critical view of screen layout remains a mystery. Could it be that users with a clear purpose in using a program are more critical of its shortcomings than less serious users?

The lack of learning from off-screen interaction among independent users is logical, as is the large amount from the whole class users. What is disappointing in relation to what is often written about group work with CALL is the negative result for group users who potentially could be benefiting more from communication off-screen with each other discussing possible answers than from working with the program *per se*. Observation showed

Table 3 Matters on which there were significant differences between modes of use

	Indep	*Group*	*Class*
Attractiveness of screen layout	3.75	1.63	1.31
Suitability of content to task	0.0	2.63	3.75
Motivating quality of computer task	3.75	5.12	6.0
Learning from off-screen interaction	6.0	5.5	0.0
Need for support material	1.88	1.88	5.25

that the talk in these groups *was* task oriented, but conducted in the native language (Greek), not English. In fact it is possible to argue that such communication is not totally worthless, since it may contribute to heightening metalinguistic awareness of features of the target language, though clearly the subjects themselves did not perceive it as having much value. Finally the class users' lack of claimed need for support material clearly arises from the fact that the active involvement of the teacher in this mode made such materials unnecessary.

Results: Further Exploration of the Data

Additional to the main analysis, exploratory correlation and cluster analyses were performed in order to further illuminate the nature of the dependent variables and subjects involved. Factor analysis was not pursued since preliminary trials showed that the data had high dimensionality, with only 29% of the variance being accounted for by the first two components (compare here the analysis in Akahori, 1988).

Correlations among dependent variables

An examination of the Pearson correlations for all subjects among responses on 27 questionnaire items showed some readily understandable tendencies. For instance, those subjects who found it easiest to get help on screen also found the instructions easy to understand ($r = 0.42$) but judged the feedback particularly inadequate ($r = -0.47$). Clearly the feedback is not perceived as unsatisfactory simply through incomprehension, therefore. Predictably those who claimed to learn most from off-screen interaction found support materials least necessary ($r = -0.45$).

Importantly for teachers organising CALL activities, subjects who found the program not suited to their own needs also judged it intrinsically uninteresting ($r = 0.42$), as did those who felt the program was incompatible with other teaching they were receiving ($r = 0.44$), who naturally also showed a low preference for computer-based learning over learning alone or with the teacher ($r = 0.59$). And if a program is uninteresting, the task done with it is not motivating ($r = 0.62$). Interestingly, those who judged the screen layout of their program particularly attractive nevertheless also found the task not motivating ($r = -0.41$). Experienced CALL users such as those in this study are no longer charmed by superficialities! And those who judged the text or words useful regardless of the activity still found the task unmotivating as well ($r = -0.44$). Clearly nothing short of complete accommodation of CALL to their own needs and other teaching will satisfy these users.

Clusters of subjects

Finally, the data was submitted to cluster analysis using the Quick Cluster option in the SPSSX statistical package. Cluster analysis identifies 'natural' groups of subjects from similarities in their patterns of response over a range of variables, without using any *a priori* groupings. In the present instance two distinct clusters were readily identifiable. Variables on which they exhibited the most marked differences are detailed in Table 4.

Table 4 Profiles of two kinds of CALL user as derived from cluster analysis of 48 subjects and 27 variables

		Clus 1	*Clus 2*
A	Ease of loading the program	0.14	3.0
	Ease of quitting the program	0.21	1.5
	Ease of repeating the program	0.21	3.0
	Ease of moving the cursor	0.64	1.5
	Ease of understanding instructions	0.68	1.75
B	Attractiveness of screen layout	2.38	0.64
	Helpfulness of colour	1.5	0.43
C	Suitability of language to student level	0.79	2.57
	Suitability of program to student age	1.41	2.36
	Suitability of content to task	1.5	5.14
D	Learning from off-screen interaction	4.59	1.71
E	Need for support material	2.47	4.29
	Number of subjects in cluster	34	14

Cluster 1 contains users who find the mechanics of using the computer exceptionally easy (A), while cluster 2 has slightly more difficulty (though not a lot in absolute terms). As a consequence, perhaps, cluster 1 exhibits greater criticism of the technical features of the computer (B) than does cluster 2. It is only when one is completely at ease working a piece of machinery that one feels in a position to criticise the way it works. Also perhaps understandably cluster 1 is more convinced of certain pedagogical qualities (C) of CALL than cluster 2, whose members have in particular a very different view of the suitability of the program contents to the learning task and correspondingly claim to learn much more from off-screen interaction (D). Cluster 1 also sees more need for support materials. There were negligible differences between the clusters on many of the crucial pedagogical variables whose correlations were discussed above: clearly on many important matters these two kinds of user agree.

In short one might describe cluster 1 as containing more 'impersonal' users, ready to rely considerably on the computer and other materials when using CALL, while cluster 2 are more 'personal', less prepared to focus on machinery and books, and looking more to interaction to learn from. To some extent this picture may be an artifact of the conditions of this study and the particular questions asked, though in fact only 10 of the 16 Class-mode users fell in cluster 2, which also contained three Group-mode users and one Independent-mode user. At least this typology of CALL users is intuitively plausible and highly suggestive. It implies that different strategies for handling CALL may be needed by teachers with users of each type.

Conclusion

The conclusion for the evaluation process itself as illustrated here is clearly that this sort of 'self-report' and observational data-gathering does produce useful information, albeit with heavy reliance on the introspective abilities of learners themselves, and a good deal of careful interpretation. Ideally it would be done in conjunction with more traditional product-focused research documenting actual achievement on linguistic variables.

The conclusions for CALL as instantiated in the situation studied are reasonably clear, and on the whole more negative than in other studies such as those cited earlier. The programmers have not done as much as is possible even with current programming to provide useful feedback, and this does not pass unnoticed with users (as Swartz, et al., 1990 also found). And the teachers are not implementing CALL optimally. They must recognise that CALL is not something to be just tacked on to a language course but that it must be made integral with what is going on in the rest of the course, in particular by use of authoring facilities. And they must realise that CALL is not so much programs as activities which need to be varied, to be suited to learners' personal needs, to be aimed at clear objectives, and to explicitly highlight the valuable off-screen interaction element. Experienced learners will not be motivated by anything less. These considerations largely swamp any simple differences between ages of learner or programs or the three modes of use contrasted. Furthermore, we have shown that not all CALL users are the same. In fact many of the points just made echo the advice of standard teacher guides to CALL such as Jones & Fortescue (1987): clearly better teacher training in this area is required.

However, in conclusion it must be stressed that this remains an evaluation of particular programs and teaching situations: it does nothing to refute the *potential* of CALL to reflect appropriate theories more adequately and be much more successful in practice.

References

Ahmed, K., Corbett, G., Rogers, M. and Sussex, R. (1985) *Computers, Language Learning and Language Teaching.* Cambridge University Press.

Akahori, K. (1988) Evaluation of educational computer software in Japan (1). *Programmed Learning and Educational Technology* 25, 46–56.

Blondel, M., Brick, N., Horricks, G. and McBride, N. (1991) Theory and reality of evaluation. *CALL* 3, 55–67.

Hamburger, H. (1990) Evaluation of L2 systems — learners and theory. *CALL* 1, 19–27.

Horton, S., Lovitt, T. and Givens, A. (1988) A computer based vocabulary program for three categories of student. *British Journal of Educational Technology* 19, 131–143.

Johnston, V. (1985) Introducing the microcomputer into English II and III. *British Journal of Educational Technology* 16, 199–218.

Jones, C. (1986) It's not so much the program, more what you do with it: The importance of methodology in CALL. *System* 14, 171–8.

Jones, C. and Fortescue, S. (1987) *Using Computers in the Language Classroom.* Longman.

Kenning, M-M. (1991) CALL evaluation — the learner's view. *CALL* 4, 21–7.

Kenning, M-M. and Kenning, M. (1990) *Computers and Language Learning: Current Theory and Practice.* Ellis Horwood.

Ng, E. and Olivier, P. (1987) Computer assisted language learning: An investigation on some design and implementation issues. *System* 15, 1–17.

Odell, A. (1986) Evaluating CALL software. In G. Leech and C. Candlin (eds) *Computers in English Language Teaching and Research.* Longman.

Phillips, M. (1987) Potential paradigms and possible problems for CALL. *System* 15, 275–87.

Poulsen, E. (1990) Evaluation of CALL from a classroom perspective. *CALL* 1, 73–8.

Scholfield, P. (1991) Language awareness and the computer. In C. James and P. Garrett (eds) *Language Awareness in the Classroom.* Longman.

Swartz, M., Kostyla, S. Hanfling, S. and Hollan, V. (1990) Preliminary assessment of a foreign language learning environment. *CALL* 1, 51–64.

Windeatt, S. (1986) Observing CALL in action. In G. Leech and and C. Candlin (eds) *Computers in English Language Teaching and Research.* Longman.

7 Narrative Analysis: Applying Linguistics to Cultural Models of Learning

MARTIN CORTAZZI, *University of Leicester*
LIXIAN JIN, *De Montfort University, Leicester*

Introduction

Everybody tells stories: jokes, ancedotes, accounts of personal experiences, and other kinds of narratives. And yet, while humanity seems to be 'homo narrans', the narratives we tell probably show cultural variation at some level or other, because narrative, as a process, is in Bruner's phrase, a 'cultural system of interpretation' (1990: 33). *Whether* and *how* we give everyday accounts of our experiences, *what* we choose to say, and *why* may vary culturally. Narrative analysis, as a research method, might therefore be used as a tool to investigate speakers' cultural perceptions on what is narrated. In this paper, we propose that an extended use of Labov's approach to narrative can be used to investigate the nature of cultural perceptions of experience. We focus on the use of narrative analysis to investigate cultural models of learning.

Our evidence is drawn from a study of narratives told by 123 British primary teachers; a second study of narratives told by 101 Chinese postgraduate students studying in Britain and by 37 of their British university supervisors; and narratives told by a further 21 Chinese postgraduates in China.

Narrative and Culture

That narrative reflects culture has been shown by a number of investigators. Tannen (1980), for example, compared the oral narratives of Greek and American women, told after viewing a silent film. The Greeks seemed to be 'acute judges', recounting events and interpreting, ascribing motives to characters and offering judgements. The Americans, on the other hand, were 'acute recallers', giving more detailed, objective reports and showing concern with time reference. Where Americans focused on content, Greeks focused on interpersonal involvement.

Another example: after collecting extensive stories of the life experiences of 100 Chinese, Zhang & Sang (1986: 368) concluded that the tellers often used one of two narrative methods, 'one is a way of talking that is not Chinese, but like the narration in Greek tragedy: starting in the middle of the story. The other is that . . . the narrators mention the key point only very briefly and then pass on, while going into great and repeated detail about common experiences in shared time and place'. The point of the narrative in this second Chinese pattern might well be missed by someone expecting it elsewhere, say at the end, as in many Western stories.

The word 'narrative' in English derives from the Latin 'gnarus', meaning knowing: in our every day stories we tell what we know or experience, or as White (1980: 1) puts it, narrative is 'the solution to a problem of general concern, namely the problem of translating knowing into telling'. If this is the process of narration, then a productive view of narrative analysis is that we analyse the telling to get back to the teller's knowing: narrative analysis can reveal not only tellers' knowledge, but also tellers' *cultural perceptions* of their experience (see Figure 1).

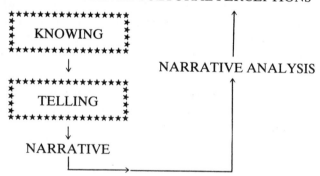

SPEAKER'S EXPERIENCE/CULTURAL PERCEPTIONS

Figure 1 Translating telling back to knowing

'Culture', here refers to the attitudes, beliefs, frameworks of interpretation and patterns of thinking and behaviour of social or ethnic groups and also those of major occupational groups, such as teachers. By analysing such occupational narratives as teachers' stories of their experiences in the classroom, for example, we can begin to distil the cultural perceptions that are presumably part of their professional experience. How teachers see children; how teachers think about children learning lessons they have taught, or classroom disasters or humorous events, can be approached through narrative analysis (Cortazzi, 1991, 1993). Similarly, cultural expectations and attitudes can be shown by looking at university tutors and students' narratives, analysing how British university tutors and supervisors see their Chinese students, their way of working, their language problems, compared with those Chinese students' perceptions of their own experience of studying in Britain, their interaction with colleagues or their social life (Jin, 1992).

Labov's model of narratives

An oral narrative of personal experience has two main functions, according to Labov (Labov & Waletsky, 1967; Labov 1972): a *referential* and an *evaluative* function. In the first, the teller gives information by referring to experience, or by recapitulating it. This is the reporting of what happened. In the second function, the teller communicates the meaning of the narrative by establishing some point of personal involvement. This is the evaluation: the speaker's perspective on what it all means. Within most personal stories, one part, at least, can usually be clearly identified as having an evaluative function. This is the Evaluation section (see below).

The extension to Labov's work is to see that in the study of occupational narrative it is crucial to know how participants see their working situation and what key events mean to them. A study of the Evaluation sections of narratives can tell us this. A large number of teachers' stories about their personal experiences can be collected on common topics. Different sections of the narrative structure can be examined for points of interest, especially the Evaluations. With due regard to context, the Evaluations of many teachers on the same topic can then be systematically compared. Similarly, we can analyse Chinese students' narratives or those of any other group, to ascertain their cultural perceptions through their own interpretations (the Evaluation) in narratives.

Labov analyses narratives as having a structure which consists of six elements, not all of which need to be present in a story. The elements are:

- Abstract
- Orientation
- Complication
- Resolution
- Evaluation
- Coda

These are briefly explained below.

The *Abstract* is at the beginning of the story. It summarises the point in advance, as a preview, or it states a general proposition that the narrative will to follow will exemplify. Like the Evaluation, the Abstract is important to an analyst, or hearer, because it indicates what the speaker thinks the story is about and shows his or her interpretation of it.

The *Orientation*, or setting, typically gives details of the time, place, situation and people involved. This is usually mentioned at the beginning of the story but is sometimes filled in later.

For researchers, the Orientation is important, because if the teller believes the hearer does not know the relevant context, sufficient background detail is provided for the narrative to be understood. Narratives thus contain sufficient contextual information to be understood as the teller intends. There is therefore some validity in collecting a large number of narratives from a large number of teachers or students in relatively brief interviews without the need to have access to detailed information about their classrooms or lives through observation or more extended interviews. In this view it is not the objective truth of the narrated events which is the focus but what narrative analysis tells us about tellers' subjective perceptions of what happened.

The *Complication* is a series of clauses in the past, or sometimes present, tense, which make up the main sequence of events in the narrative. this is the basic content. It commonly includes a problem, dilemma, change or something newsworthy which gives the story interest.

The *Resolution* describes the outcome, solution or result of problems presented in the Complication. Some narratives have inconclusive results where problems remain unresolved. In others, the resolution of one problem itself leads to a further problem, so that the narrative takes the form of cycles of Complications and Resolutions.

The *Evaluation* underlines the point of the narrative, revealing the speaker's attitude to what has been recounted and how the teller thinks it should be interpreted. Evaluations may be distributed at any point in the narrative and they may overlap with other structures. Many Evaluations occur at the end of a story. The Evaluation wards off the withering rejoinder of 'So what?' — 'Every good narrator is constantly warding off this question' (Labov *et al.*, 1968: 287). Storytellers use many different ways to evaluate narratives (Labov *et al.*, 1968: 301–4; Labov, 1972: 370–5). Essentially the Evaluation is marked off from the rest of the narrative by explicit interpretation of the teller or through the words of a character in the story; by rhetorical underlining with exclamations, repetition, heavy use of adjectives or adverbs; by using gesture, special intonation or pitch range. 'Narratives do not merely inform: they convey the importance of the narrated events and tell how those events should be interpreted and weighed by the listener' (Peterson & McCabe, 1983: 60). The Evaluation 'reveals the attitude of the narrator towards the narrative by emphasizing the relative importance of some narrative units as opposed to others' (Labov & Waletsky, 1967: 37). 'Unevaluated narratives lack structural definition' (ibid: 39).

The *Coda* brings the listeners back to the present time and concludes the narrative, often by using a formulaic phrase, such as 'That was that' or 'So there you are'.

The above structures do not necessarily follow this canonical order; additional information for an orientation or a complication may come later in a narrative or at several points. Not all elements necessarily occur in a narrative.

Labov's model has been applied to literary analysis (Platt, 1977; Carter & Simpson, 1982; Maclean, 1988), to analysing children's writing in education (Taylor, 1986), to developmental psycholinguistics (Kernan, 1977; Peterson & McCabe, 1983), mass communications (van Dijk, 1987, 1988) and anthropology (Watson, 1973), but not — so far as we know — to analysing cultural perceptions (Cortazzi, 1991, 1993).

Extension of Labov's model to analyse cultural perceptions

The key to our use of Labov's model of narrative analysis is that in the Evaluation the speaker highlights the meaning of the narrative and the reason for telling it. The Evaluation is the speaker's interpretation of the personal experience reported in the narrative. Therefore, if a number of narratives on similar topics are collected from speakers of the same occupation, social or ethnic group, the Evaluation sections of the narratives can be analysed in order to distil the tellers' cultural perceptions of the incidents narrated. In this way, Cortazzi (1991) analysed one thousand narratives of British primary teachers and was able to present a picture of their cultural perception of key aspects of their work. Following this example, Jin (1992) analysed narratives of British supervisors and Chinese students which appeared in interviews to examine their cultural orientations to each other and perceptions in British and Chinese academic cultures. A narrative told by a British supervisor illustrates such a cultural perception:

A . . . Chinese students can put up much better with loneliness, being away from home and not having their girlfriend with them or family there.

O I mean, I had one Chinese research student, he was very good student

C and he came over and left his girlfriend for three years and I found this very hard how he would cope with it

R but he managed.

E But again he had this tremendous . . ., he wanted the Ph.D., he wanted to get the training and he was willing to sacrifice. Now not many other races in my experience will do that.

The speaker perceives Chinese students as having the social and psychological problem of loneliness, being homesick and lacking family life or personal relationships. He understands that they cope very well with such difficulties and are willing to make sacrifices for their degrees, training or career, as others might not do. Apparently, this demonstrates their determination, which reflects the impact of traditional Chinese values of study and academic achievement, even though this means sacrificing, for a time, the traditional closeness of the family.

From the Chinese side, such study is considered a very respectable activity, as shown in a popular traditional saying: 'Thousands of professions and activities are at the lower level while only *study* is considered to be at the highest'. The relationship between the value of study and family closeness depends on the cultural values in a society. In China, this unique and hard-won opportunity of studying abroad is given priority over family closeness as a matter of course because of the deep-rooted value given to study. The sacrifice therefore has a strong social justification; it is expected of everyone capable of higher study. Given the collective orientation of Chinese culture this may make the sacrifice relatively easier, while to more individually-oriented Western eyes, it seems that the individual is sacrificing much. Chinese, to whom we have shown this narrative, do not even consider it a particularly good example to show the determination and motivation of Chinese students. They take the sacrifice for granted: studying is a priority and the normal expectation is that through such study a person will be in a better position to establish a career and hence help the family later. Yet it is likely that a British supervisor sees the value differently according to his cultural or personal evaluation.

The following example, recounted by a British supervisor, illustrates a perception of British academic culture.

A I got trapped into virtually writing the essays of some of the students.

O They would say 'would I look at it?'

C and I had such difficulty in making sense with what they had written that I ended up writing it myself in between the lines

R but I stopped doing that. My style is to say, 'Well, I'm not going to give you a title because I don't know what is going on in your mind and in your professional and personal experience.

E It is a Master's degree course, after all, and if that doesn't include personal autonomy then what's the point?'

The British tutor explicitly states here that a student who is going to get a higher degree ought to develop personal autonomy. The narrative is structured to build up to this Evaluation. In the teller's perception, giving too much help prevents students acquiring academic independence. Such autonomy, however, is not necessarily required or emphasised in other cultures.

Another narrative demonstrates a Chinese student's worry about relationships with authority, in this case a British Dean in his department.

A I spoke out what I thought.

C But it was awkward when I came here at the beginning.

O I wanted to change the research direction, so I had to change supervisor. When I talked to the Dean,

C he vaguely suggested that I shouldn't change. but he also said he could allow me to change if I insisted on it.

R Eventually I decided to transfer here.

E Now this Dean is obviously not happy and offended. He doesn't greet me when he sees me, ignoring me completely.

The Complication of this narrative illustrates a cultural difficulty: the question of where the main emphasis lies. It is likely that the Dean's main idea was expressed first, that the student shouldn't change supervisors. His second quoted statement may well have been a 'softener' or let-out clause. The student seems to have interpreted it otherwise, that the Dean's main point is that he can change and that the opening statement is merely a polite preliminary to saying so.

There are several possible explanations for the lack of greeting, which seems to worry the teller. It could be, as the narrator felt, that changing research direction and supervisor caused a bad relationship with the departmental authority. It could be his misjudgement and misinterpretation of the Dean's social manner and approach. It could be that the Dean simply did not see him and therefore did not greet him, although the student believed he was seen by the Dean and felt ignored. To a British person this might have no particular significance. In China, a leader showing his awareness and recognition of the existence of a junior person is an important signal of security and honour to the latter, and witholding such recognition could be demeaning, especially to a visiting scholar or a researcher, who might be quite senior in his own country.

A more likely interpretation — for the speaker — is the Chinese assumption that going against the wishes of an authority might cause a bad relationship (as in a Chinese context), for the leader might think the student's action had disturbed the harmony of the original team and that he disobeyed what a senior person had suggested. However, in a British academic context, even if a Dean had been unhappy with the change, it is normal and acceptable for a request for such a change to be granted if there are valid reasons. It is unlikely that a British Dean would be involved personally and emotionally in the matter, nor would he be likely to interpret the event in terms of destabilising harmonic relationships.

Furthermore, this Chinese student seems to blame this bad relationship on his outspoken manner, which, he probably believed, was acceptable in Britain as a form of directness or being straightforward. Yet he was disappointed by what he thought he experienced by speaking out. This might make him believe that this kind of offence, as it might be taken to be in China, occurs in Britain as well. This may give him extra worries about relationships, which Chinese people care for enormously, apart from the normal concerns about learning how to express their wishes in a style appropriate to British academic culture.

The narrative examples shown above demonstrate thinking or perceptions of British tutors and Chinese students on various aspects of academic life. These perceptions can be seen particularly in the stages of Abstract and Evaluation of a narrative. The rest of a narrative is the story of personal experience chosen by the narrator to lead to or build up to the points he or she wants to make, although the choice of a story also illustrates some cultural values of the narrator.

Cultural Models of Learning Expressed by Narratives

Out of nearly a thousand narratives told by British primary teachers in our data, 96 focus on directly on children's learning. These have been analysed to show, first, that the 'breakthrough' is an important model of learning for teachers, though not the only one; second, many narratives about learning have key metaphors in the evaluation sections; third, underlying structures and perceptions in these narratives about learning expressed by British teachers and Chinese students can be further illustrated in the form of a semiotic square. Finally, Chinese cultural perspectives on the use of questions in learning are demonstrated. Each of these will be discussed in turn.

The breakthrough as a model of learning

Two examples of a primary teacher's narratives follow. A teacher describes breakthroughs in children's learning. This kind of narrative can be analysed to reveal cultural models of learning.

O   One boy that I've had a lot of trouble with,
        his reading is not good, but his number was appalling.
C   He couldn't count, he couldn't recognize any numbers and then
R/E   all of a sudden in the space of about two weeks
        it seemed to click and I could see him beginning to go.
Coda He's now beginning to understand it.
E   It suddenly came on.
O   And then another little boy who just did not understand addition at all,
C   I tried it all ways. You name it, I tried it
R/E   and then all of a sudden he just came in one day
        and [clicks fingers] *it seemed to click* and I could really see the break-
        through.

Such accounts could easily be dismissed as anecdotal — interesting but
unimportant slices of classroom life, small experiences of the tellers which
do not count for much in research terms. However, when a large number of
such narratives are collected and analysed — independently and spontane-
ously told by different teachers in different schools — it becomes clear that
there are common patterns in both the content and in the ways of telling.
One way to analyse the data is to take out different sections of the narratives,
the Evaluations, for example, and see if there are frequently occurring elements. In fact, this reveals that the teachers describe the key moment of
learning in characteristic ways.

Metaphors in narratives

The actual moment of learning is typically described in images: a large
number of teachers repeatedly use a limited range of metaphors at the Evaluation points in their narratives. From 96 breakthrough narratives, the following
occur in the Evaluations.

No fewer than 28 narratives portray learning as a CLICK. Such phrases
as 'it clicks', 'it all clicked', 'it seemed to click', 'there was a sort of click in
their minds', 'it must have just clicked' seem remarkably common. Eighteen
narratives depict learning as LIGHT: 'the light dawns', 'daylight has dawned
at last', 'he saw the light', 'her face lit up', 'this sort of flash going straight
through'. Fifty narratives show learning as MOVEMENT: 'he just came on',
'she's just come out', 'they've come through', 'they're not going to move that
much', 'they all seemed to be moving', 'she just goes straight through', 'she's
gone'. Some of these are vigorous images of flight: 'we really have got lift off
point with her', 'they take off again', 'this girl has suddenly taken off'; or of
speed: 'she was running away with her reading', 'he whipped through', 'they
zoomed away', 'they had a surge'.

The model of learning which can be distilled from these stories about breakthroughs in children's learning is that there is first a struggle with learning: the teacher tries various methods but the learner is so far unsuccessful. In the narratives the teller often shares thoughts or feelings about this which reportedly occurred to him or her at the time. Then something 'clicks' or 'light dawns'. This happens suddenly, or at least, it is noticed suddenly. Then there is a moment of joy, where again the teller is very likely to share thoughts and emotions about the event. The teacher expresses surprise, amazement and wonder and thinks that this is what makes teaching worthwhile and rewarding — it is worth the struggle.

Figure 2 Teachers' perceptions of breakthroughs in learning

There's a struggle

Teachers saw the period before the breakthrough as a struggle. 'They struggle with it for day after day.' It was an 'uphill struggle', 'such a struggle at first'. The child was 'struggling away', having 'tremendous difficulty' 'having a lot of trouble', 'not making any headway', 'struggling with her reading'. 'You struggle for months, you struggle, I struggle, everybody struggles with this child and we're almost on the verge of despair when it clicks.'

It's a thrill

Teachers' reactions were that the breakthrough was 'amazing', 'fantastic', 'smashing', 'terrific', 'marvellous'. They were thrilled: 'it gives you the greatest thrill', 'I was thrilled about that', 'I was so thrilled when she got it right', 'He was thrilled and I was thrilled'. 'I said how thrilled I was. I *was* thrilled', 'I was thrilled to bits with her. That truly is your breakthrough and that gives you a tremendous thrill.'

This is what makes it worthwhile

The breakthrough, small though it may appear, constitutes part of a major professional reward. 'That moment makes everything worthwhile.' 'You can't put a worth on it in financial terms.' 'That gives me a real thrill, that really makes it a worthwhile job.' It is 'very rewarding'. It is 'where you get the most satisfaction'. It gives 'tremendous satisfaction' and is 'a satisfying worthwhile experience'. It is 'what makes me feel I've achieved something'. It is 'where the fulfilment of teaching comes from'. It is 'the joy and satisfaction of your job, when a child . . . you give them a new concept and they struggle with it for day after day and you're thinking of different ways round it and suddenly it clicks. The job's worthwhile. You're doing a worthwhile job and I feel that that is what makes the job'.

Thoughts

In narratives, before the 'click' the teachers share their thoughts: 'I thought, "My God, this child is never going to get off on his reading".' 'You think, "Oh, I'll never do anything with them".' 'You think, "Oh dear, so and so is going to know absolutely nothing".'

After the 'click', they also reported their thoughts: 'I thought, "major breakthrough!".' I thought, "Great, we've got through at last!".' 'I thought, "We've got somewhere at last!".' 'I thought, "My God, he's progressed!".' 'I really thought, "We've made it!".' 'I think, "My God, he's writing stories and they make sense".' 'I think, "Smashing, you're doing a good job with her".'

Whether the teachers really thought these things at the time, or whether they are, like Greek storytellers, highlighting the drama of the telling by reporting thoughts as direct quotations (Tannen, 1989: 126) is not clear. Both are possible.

The Function of Metaphors in Narrative

This kind of model of learning is illustrated by two further stories which are built around metaphors.

O   One particular girl,
C   she suddenly realised she was making headway and
R   the whole of her outlook on school work changed dramatically because of that, and *her achievements went up in leaps and bounds.*
E   it may have had something to do with teacher expectations as well.
R   She has suddenly *taken off* with her reading and other things.
R/E I was sat there, I must have looked daft because I had a silly grin all over my face and I was so pleased with this and that was my reward for the day, that she had achieved and that she had somehow managed to get herself going. I think any little thing that a child doesn't understand and

is genuinely worried about and comes to you and says to you, 'I don't understand this. I can't make head or tail of it'. And if they go away and they can understand it, you can see the *light dawn on their face* and that to me is worth — well, you can't put a worth on it in financial terms.

A   You get lots of small instances. I think you share in the child's delight in that.

O   I can think of lots of little instances

C   where you've been plugging away, particularly with reading, sometimes with writing, where they've struggled, you've helped and you've felt for months and months that you've made very little progress

R/E and suddenly it *dawns* on you that the child is improving. Suddenly the reading is coming on, the smile that *dawns* on that child's face when they appreciate that they can read. It's a most exciting moment.

It is evident that metaphors for children's learning and understanding are frequently used by primary teachers in Breakthrough narratives. These metaphors occur predominantly in the Resolution section of this group of narratives, i.e. where the actual moment of a child's understanding is described. The metaphors can also be seen as having an Evaluative function since the narrator is recounting an evaluative action (cf. Labov's examples, 'He turned white', 'She was shaking like a leaf', 1972: 371). There is a notable absence of terminology from educational psychology or learning theory. The explanation is wrapped in metaphor.

It might be tempting to interpret the use of these metaphors as a poetic response by teachers to the magic of the moment. Such an interpretation would take a 'classical' view of metaphor as a departure from ordinary modes of language for purposes of decorative addition. However, many twentieth century writers have commented that metaphor is not ornamental, but is central to language, defining and refining it (Hawkes, 1972: 67). Metaphor is seen as the basis of conceptual systems (Lakoff & Johnson, 1980; Salmond, 1982; Taylor, 1984). Metaphors pervade ordinary talk and are systematically organised in clusters, typically exemplified in the common Western metaphors of 'Argument is war' and 'Time is money' (Lakoff & Johnson, 1980) or 'Knowledge is a landscape' (Salmond, 1982) around both of which many everyday metaphorical expressions are grouped. 'The most fundamental values in a culture will be coherent with the metaphorical structure of the most fundamental concepts in the culture' (Lakoff & Johnson, 1980: 22).

One way of attempting to analyse the patterns of values which occur in narratives is to distil them into semiotic squares.

Perceptions of Learning Through Semiotic Squares

In a semiotic square, horizontal dimensions are contraries, vertical ones are complementaries and diagonal ones are contradictory. Figure 3 summarises aspects of primary teachers' perceptions of classroom learning, as seen in their narratives.

Figure 3 Teachers' perceptions of key aspects of learning

Teachers invariably affirm that they plan classroom work but many narratives are all about flexibility: the teacher responds immediately to the children's interest and enjoyment when things 'crop up'. Learning combines both planning and flexibility: much learning is planned, yet the more memorable instances of learning and the most successful lessons reported in narratives come from the teacher's flexible response to children's reactions — 'playing it by ear'. A breakthrough involves neither planning nor flexibility since narratives reveal the fortuitous, sudden, unpredictable nature of the breakthrough, yet breakthroughs are not exploited for children's interests in the way in which things which 'crop up' are treated. A breakthrough is only one kind of learning but it is apparently outside the teacher's control.

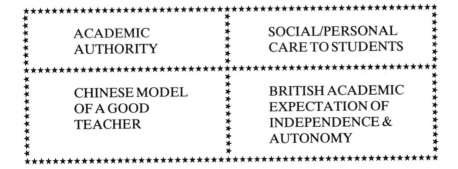

Figure 4 Contrasting perceptions of the role of the teacher

A second square shows the Chinese students' expectations of teachers, as revealed by the students' narratives. Teachers should, in this view, have academic authority. They should be experts in their field and a source of knowledge. Students expect that this knowledge will be transmitted in the classroom. Teachers should also show care and concern to students in a parental role which is quite different to that of dispensing knowledge. The combination of these make up the main features of the Chinese model of a good teacher. However, Chinese students find neither of these in British academic life: teachers encourage intellectual autonomy and therefore wish learners to find out for themselves. They will give *some* information and knowledge, but only enough to start learners on their own path, especially with research students. Few British university teachers seem to think that they have a major social, pastoral or 'parental' role for students, even within a tutorial system. British cultural expectations differ from Chinese ones in these respects.

Perspectives on Students' Questions in Learning

A specific instance of these kinds of differences is found for questions — *whether, how* and *why* students might ask questions. A British perspective is that questions are a means of learning. Students ask questions in order to find out information. Teachers therefore encourage students to ask for heuristic reasons: the more you ask the more you may know. Questions have the interactive function of engendering discussion and are therefore important in a seminar approach to learning, which stresses that through talking one learns. Questions may also show the quality of thinking, so teachers may encourage learners to ask for diagnostic motives, so that they know what and how students are thinking. For these kinds of reasons students are encouraged to ask questions as a means of learning.

The analysis of Chinese students' narratives shows a somewhat different perspective. As they explain in their Evaluations, students will only ask questions under specific circumstances, for example *after* a class. There is a strong tendency *not* to ask questions, for at least five reasons.

First, questions may disturb the class. 'In China, the most important thing is to listen and be attentive. You have to learn and be attentive. You have to learn and remember.' If you ask questions, 'You will disturb or interrupt the teacher and you may disturb the other students'. In China there are usually a large number of students in the classroom, so that this presents a numerical constraint: the larger the group, the greater the tendency for individuals to keep silent.

Second, the questioner will feel embarrassed. He or she 'will feel foolish, supposing that all the other students understand'. Therefore, questioners risk losing face.

Third, the students do not want to present problems for the teacher. If the teacher cannot answer, or is slow to answer, then the teacher will lose face: the student who causes this to happen also loses face by publicly lowering the respect which should be shown to the teacher. 'Perhaps they can't react quickly so they will look foolish and that's very bad for the teacher. They always want to avoid that.'

Fourth, a good teacher, in the Chinese view, will predict the students' questions. 'A Chinese teacher anticipates students' questions. He prepares an explanation with the anticipated questions in mind so that they don't need to ask.' If a student asks a question which the teacher has not predicted, then the teacher may not be able to answer and again loses face.

Fifth, if a student has a question it is probably not important. The reason for this is that a good teacher should explain the important points anyway, so if the point the student has in mind is not explained it cannot be important. 'A good teacher will anticipate that students will ask a question and during his talking he will explain it later so we don't ask the question, we just wait and sometime later I think the teacher will explain it.' 'A good teacher will know which parts of his subject will cause the students to have problems and he will explain those parts carefully, so if there is a part which you don't understand it doesn't matter. The problems which the teacher doesn't explain aren't important.'

This perspective effectively vetoes most questions. The would-be questioner probably waits till after the class to ask or tries to find the answer in the library, although this may depend on the age of the teacher. 'The young teachers will answer you — after a fashion. But the older ones, they'll say, "Just keep it till after the class and I'll tell you".'

We hope we have shown that analysing the narratives collected in recorded discussions and interviews can be a fruitful approach to investigating cultural perspectives.

References

Bruner, J. (1990) *Acts of Meaning*. Cambridge, MA: Harvard University Press.
Carter, R. and Simpson, P. (1982) The sociolinguistic analysis of narrative. *Belfast Working Papers in Linguistics* 6, 123–52.
Cortazzi, M. (1991) *Primary Teaching: How it is, a Narrative Account*. London: David Fulton.

— (1993) *Narrative Analysis*. London: Falmer Press.

van Dijk, T. A. (1987) *Communicating Racism, Ethnic Prejudice in Thought and Talk*. London: Sage.

— (1988) *News as Discourse*. Hillsdale, NJ: Lawrence Erlbaum.

Hawkes, T. (1972) *Metaphor*. London: Methuen.

Jin, L. (1992) *Academic Cultural Expectations and Second Language Use: Chinese Postgraduate Students in the UK — A Cultural Synergy Model*. Unpublished PhD thesis. University of Leicester.

Labov, W. (1972) The transformation of experience in narrative Syntax. In W. Labov *Language in the Inner City* (pp. 352–96). Philadelphia: University of Pennsylvania.

Labov, W., Cohen, P., Robins, C. and Lewis, J. (1968) *A Study of the Non-Standard English of Negro and Puerto-Rican Speakers in New York City* Vol. 2. Washington, CD: Office of Education, US Dept of Health, Education and Welfare.

Labov, W. and Waletsky, J. (1967) Narrative analysis: Oral versions of personal experience. In J. Helm (ed.) *Essays on the Verbal and Visual Arts* (pp. 12–44). Seattle: American Ethnological Society.

Lakoff, G. and Johnson, M. (1980) *Metaphors We Live By*. Chicago: University of Chicago Press.

Kernan, K. T. (1977) Semantic and Expressive Elaboration in Children's Narratives. In S. Ervin-Tripp (ed.) *Child Discourse* (pp. 91–102). New York: Academic Press.

Maclean, M. (1988) *Narrative as Performance, a Beaudelairian Experiment*. London: Routledge.

Peterson, C. and McCabe, A. (1983) *Developmental Psycholinguistics, Three Ways of Looking at a Child's Narrative*. New York: Plenum Press.

Platt, M. L. (1977) *Towards a Speech Act Theory of Literary Analysis*. Bloomington: Indiana University Press.

Salmond, A. (1982) Theoretical Landscapes, on Cross-cultural Perceptions of Knowledge. In D. Parkin (ed.) *Semantic Anthropology* (pp. 65–87). London: Academic Press.

Tannen, D. (1980) A comparative analysis of oral narrative strategies: Athenian Greek and American English. In W. L. Chafe (ed.) *The Pear Stories: Cognitive, Cultural and Linguistic Aspects of Narrative Production* (pp. 51–87). Norwood, New Jersey: Ablex.

— (1989) *Talking Voices, Repetition, Dialogue and Imagery in Conversational Discourse*. Cambridge: Cambridge University Press.

Taylor, G. (1986) The development of style in children's fictional narrative. In A. Wilkinson (ed.) *The Writing of Writing*. Milton Keynes: Open University Press.

Taylor, W. (ed.) (1984) *Metaphors of Education*. London: Heinemann.

Watson, K. A. (1973) A rhetorical and sociolinguistic analysis of narrative. *American Anthropologist* 75, 243–64.

White, H. (1980) The value of narrativity in the representation of reality. In W. J. T. Mitchell (ed.) *On Narrative* (pp. 1–49). Chicago: University of Chicago Press.

Zhang, X. and Sang, Y. (1986) *Chinese Profiles*. Beijing: Panda Books.

8 Assessing Spontaneous Language Abilities of Aphasic Speakers

SUSAN EDWARDS and RAYMOND KNOTT
University of Reading[1]

Introduction

Aphasia is an acquired language disorder which affects the speaker's ability to produce and understand spoken and written language. All parts of the language system are vulnerable: the repertoire of, or access to, phonological form, the lexicon and syntax may be variously impaired. The observation of different patterns of damage has led to the currently criticised notion of sub-categories or syndromes although the two contrasting conditions of fluent versus non-fluent aphasia are generally agreed to have both theoretical and clinical validity. Aphasia is caused by cortical damage and usually follows vascular lesions (strokes), tumours, head injuries or degenerative neurological diseases. Elderly people are most at risk although it is found in all age groups. While psychologists and linguists are showing an increasing interest in this condition, in the UK the assessment and rehabilitation of aphasic speakers is primarily the responsibility of speech and language therapists. In this paper, we report on a research project which aims to achieve a more detailed characterisation of aphasic speech collected from a range of aphasic speakers (see also Edwards, Garman & Knott, 1992a, b). For illustration we focus on one aphasic subject and compare data collected from our assessment procedures with that obtained via a widely used clinical assessment, and demonstrate how our approach reveals features of the speaker's grammatical abilities which are not exposed by the clinical assessment (for further details of assessment and treatment of this subject see Edwards, forthcoming).

The subject quoted in this paper, is a 54-year-old male (MG), with a managerial post at the time of his sudden and devastating stroke. He was left with minimal physical signs but a profound language deficit which affected both output and comprehension of spoken and written language. Classically, this type of aphasia is known as fluent aphasia as the speaker produces quantities of fluent speech although often it may, to a greater or lesser degree, lack meaning. Fluent aphasics characteristically have profound difficulty in accessing the required word, a feature which is captured in the text below and the score given in Table 1.

The following text can stand as an example of aphasic speech: the speaker MG, is describing a cartoon story which shows a couple preparing for a dinner party. The text is given without punctuation and before segmentation and the therapist's contributions are marked and given on separate lines.

Picture description

I think this chap was writing and he said hello said hello and he said I'm going to a [gate] [PARA] at twenty past seven he said ok right away and so X on they went and they were X writing there and she's getting the flowers and the {f} {f} X

THERAPIST you don't mean flowers to you
no

THERAPIST cooking

cooking cooking cooking and out there was a beautiful fish fish fish and so he went over this and he he he [lent] [PARA] this and all those lovely the {f} fish and the {f} {f} p potatoes and {f} candles and and {f} candles and candles and wine wine and so they went back and said ok and so they went upstairs and he was getting there

[gate] PARA = paraphasic error; {f} = filled pause; X = unintelligible

The aphasic speaker is able to access visual information but has severe difficulty conveying this information. He substitutes real words, uses non-words (both classified as paraphasic errors) and has difficulty in constructing a narrative. One of the clinician's primary tasks is to assess, test or describe and quantify these difficulties. We will consider how this might be achieved using our descriptive procedures.

Assessment Through Tests

Traditional assessments of spoken output (for example, The Boston Aphasia Diagnostic Examination: Goodglass & Kaplan, 1983; The Western

Aphasia Battery: Kertesz, 1982), consist of tests which measure tasks such as naming ability, repetition, picture description and to a very limited degree, conversation. However, although the examiner is expected to observe spontaneous speech, no consistent procedures are given for reliably quantifying the speech elicited. Such tests do, however, include a number of verbal subtests which the clinician can score. An example, of scores from the Boston Diagnostic Aphasia Examination (Goodglass & Kaplan, 1983), which was administered on a number of occasions to MG, is given below in Table 1. The subtests vary in length from 10 to 114 items: for ease of comparison the scores are presented here as proportions. Normal adults would be expected to score 100% on all tasks.

Table 1 Boston Diagnostic Aphasia Examination

Date of test:	7/90	10/90	2/91	8/92
Comprehension				
word discrimination	0.82	0.83	0.90	0.86
body parts	0.75	0.70	0.80	0.95
commands	0.26	0.33		0.33
Repetition				
words	0.7	1.0	0.9	1.0
phrases	0.2			0.2
Speech				
responsive naming	0.33	0.6		0.30
visual confrontational naming	0.03	0.49	0.53	0.71

We observe from the first assessment that both comprehension and expression are affected; that he is better able to understand single words than commands; and that he has great difficulty in producing single words (crucially nouns) following an auditory or visual stimulus. Retesting two years later reveals some improvement in most sections but a dramatic improvement in his confrontational naming ability (that is, naming a pictured or real object or action).

However, what this assessment fails to tell us is whether this improvement has also occurred in his conversational speech. The primary target of these types of assessment is not conversational speech although, for most, if not all speakers, it is the ability to converse with others which is most important. The importance of conversational speech also concerns others. When family or carers ask if the aphasic speaker has improved, their prime concern is with conversational speech. Now, it may be that there is a correlation between improvement on test scores (for example, confrontational naming) and improved conversational speech but this has yet to be demonstrated. To date we can record performance on standard assessments but there is not an agreed methodology for calibrating change in naturalistic speech. In order to measure improvement, we need to have a reliable methodology for collecting, analysing and quantifying naturalistic speech. During the last decade there have been a small number of studies (Penn & Behrmann, 1986; Saffran, Berndt & Schwartz, 1989; Vermeulen, Bastiaanse & Van Wageningen, 1989) which have focused on developing procedures that will provide quantitative descriptions of continuous speech of aphasics. The work reported here furthers this approach and also builds on earlier work within the department of Linguistic Science at the University of Reading which developed procedures for transcribing and analysing certain features of child language (for example, Fletcher *et al.*, 1986; Fletcher & Garman, 1988).

A Descriptive Framework for the Analysis of Spontaneous Speech

Our current project extends the procedures developed in this earlier work and focuses on capturing and quantifying syntactic and lexical features of recorded adult speech. The data have been collected from aphasic and normal speakers and consist of samples of conversational and monologic speech. Our long-term aims are to produce a methodology for transcribing, segmenting and analysing conversational speech; to compile profiles illustrating a range of aphasic features; to compare the aphasic profiles with those obtained from normal controls. A high priority has been given to the methodology we employ. In particular we aim to achieve consistent elicitation, transcription and segmentation procedures. Standard elicitation procedures are used which consist of two topic-directed conversations and two story-telling tasks one of which has pictorial support. The samples collected enable us to make within (comparing data from different elicitation tasks), as well as between subject comparisons. Audio-recordings are orthographically transcribed and segmented according to our detailed grammatical criteria.

No sensible comparisons between aphasic speakers, between speech produced on different tasks or between aphasic speakers and normal speakers can be made until reliable criteria are established for identifying the units which are to be analysed. The first task, therefore, is to establish units of text for analysis: we call these units *text units* which are based on clauses. Separate lines are used for each text unit but also for non-clausal utterances such as phrasal, lexical; and for non-productive units such as greetings, vocatives, etc. which we term *minor units*. It is important to note that as we are seeking a grammatical description of output we are aiming to create grammatically defined units for analysis rather than 'utterances' which tend to be poorly defined. Having segmented the data into text units for analysis, these units are then coded as minor, lexical, phrasal or clausal, according to their structure, and the grammatical and lexical constituents tagged. Two computerised programs are applied to give measures such as the total number of text units, types of text units and totals of types and tokens of word class and grammatical structures. These procedures deal with the well-formed utterances of both the aphasic subjects and the controls but we also need to take account of normal and aphasic speech errors. These problem units are dealt with in the following way: we log units which are incomplete and units which are not construable because they contain unintelligible elements: stereotypic expressions, repetitions and paraphasias are also tagged. Thus errors as well as preserved features of output may be quantified.

The text given above will then have the format illustrated in Figure 1.

Analysis

We can now see how the segmentation separates units for analysis and quantification. The first level of analysis, the units analysis, enables us to compare the proportion of different types of text units (minor, lexical, phrasal or clausal) used and to separate these units from those which are incomplete or unintelligible. This first sweep through the data may reveal differences both between speakers (in the example given here, an aphasic and a normal speaker) and the same speaker over time (see Table 2). At this level we observe marked differences between our two speakers.

Startling differences are apparent between the aphasic and the normal speaker when we examine the proportion of well-formed grammatical units versus single-world, minor units and unclear units. This last category includes incomplete units and units which are not construable because they contain unintelligible elements (unanalysable units). As well as differences in the amount of well formed units, we can also identify frank errors in the data. For this analysis we have logged omission of main clausal constituents, paraphasic errors and repetitions. A comparison of recordings of MG made at two different times, suggests an improvement of his control as there has been a reduction of errors on this task over time (see Table 3).

Text units	Unit type	
I think	C	
this chap was writing	C	*
and he said hello	C	
said hello	C	
and he said	C	
I'm going to a [gate] [PARA]	C	*
at twenty past seven	P	*
and he said ok right away	C	
and so X	U	
on they went	C	
and they were X	U	
writing	L	
there	L	*
and she's getting the flowers	C	
and the {f} {f} X	U	
no	M	
(cooking cooking) cooking	L	
and out there was a beautiful (fish fish) fish	C	
and so he went over this	C	
and (he he) he [lent] [PARA] this	C	
and all those lovely	I	
the {f} fish and (the) the {f} {f} p potatoes and {f} candles (and) and {f} candles and candles and (wine) wine	P	
and so they went back	C	
and said ok	C	
so they went upstairs	C	
and he was getting there	C	

C = clausal; P = phrasal; L = lexical; U = unintelligible; I = incomplete; M = minor utterance.
* = higher order grouping.

Figure 1 Transcription of taped example following segmentation procedures

Table 2 Analysis of texts produced by an aphasic and a normal speaker. Unit analysis: 100 TUs.

	Aphasic speaker		Normal control	
	12/90	*8/92*	*c/s*	*con*
clausal	39	42	69	77
phrasal	13	10	14	8
lexical	6	14	5	4
minor	12	3	9	9
unclear	30	23	3	2
% of TUs in clausal or phrasal constructions:				
	52	52	83	85

c/s = description of cartoon story.
con = conversation.

Table 3 Analysis of errors produced by an aphasic speaker. Errors in 100 TU.

	Aphasic		Control
	12/90	*8/92*	*c/s*
omissions	2	3	0
paraphasias	13	5	0
unintelligible	11	6	0
incomplete	19	16	3
% of all utterances containing an error:			
	45	30	3

A number of further analyses are usually desirable. Clausal constituents are tagged and types and tokens of clausal structures examined in order to achieve a measure of the range of clausal structures used: in a similar way, lexical tagging permits quantification of lexical diversity. An additional level of analysis explores the grammatical relationships between units and thereby permits observation of the differences subjects employ to link grammatical units. Data on these last two analyses are not explored in this paper but will be published at a later date.

Discussion

First, we will discuss the methodoogy of the project and the advantages of this type of analysis. Secondly, we will examine the data from our subject MG and show how this analysis has revealed aspects about his aphasia which are not revealed by the standard assessment procedures.

Elicitation tasks

Traditional aphasia assessments make substantial use of visual stimuli. The advantage of these tasks is that the clinician knows the intended target and can therefore identify errors. The disadvantage is that the type of speech elicited is unlikely to replicate normal conversation. In contrast, free conversation is less easy to control and errors are more difficult to identify. We have reached some sort of compromise by including a cartoon picture description task and by using a constrained format for the conversation. These methods produce larger chunks of continuous speech thereby allowing both clausal and non-clausal structures to be used and although the speech elicited may not replicate normal conversation, we maintain that it gives a reasonably representative sample. Further, the elicitation procedures have been found to be acceptable by the normal controls as well as the aphasic subjects.

Segmentation and analyses

The procedures provide us with principled criteria for segmenting the data which in turn permit us to establish a measure of productivity as well as giving a basis for comparing a range of grammatical features. As well as looking at the total number of unit types and the proportion of these which have an internal grammatical structure, we are able to examine the various combinations of clausal constituents and gain a profile of the types of TUs employed by each speaker. We are also able to examine text structure by examining the deployment of a range of grammatical linking devices. We identify a number of such devices including co-ordination, subordination, relativisation, and ellipsis. Identification and quantification of these is revealing some hitherto unobserved differences between certain types of aphasic and normal speech. These grammatical relationships between text units (intergrammatical relationships) and the groupings (higher order groupings) give us an index of grammatical complexity in addition to the length of clausal unit. Our procedures also permit us to examine the diversity of lexical class usage and to investigate diversity within a given class. All these measures permit comparisons to be made with normal controls and hence will enable us to establish severity of impairment as well as change over time.

Insights gained from MG's scores

Some of the scores obtained by these methods from MG, the aphasic subject, show marked differences when compared with scores from the normal speaker and some differences of MG's output over time.

Productivity

In the first sample he produced 39 TUs (the rest were taken from a similar task): 18 months later he easily produces over 100 TUs. Of course, an increase of TUs produced does not necessarily indicate improved output for the normal control produced an accurate and coherent account of the cartoon picture story in 70 TUs. There are, however, some types of aphasia where increased productivity would indicate improvement.

Distribution of unit types

In Table 2 we can see that MG's proportion of clausal and phrasal units is considerably lower compared with the normal speaker. Most strikingly we see that MG's proportion of phrasal and clausal constructions remains at approximately 52% of the total TUs while the control's output, regardless of task consists, consists mainly of phrasal or clausal units.

MG produces a large proportion of unclear units (30%) or units containing unintelligible elements (23%) while the control rarely produces any.

Change over time

We have noted that MG's ability to name pictured objects and actions improved as measured by the standard aphasia assessment. The unit analysis also shows an increase in the number of lexical units used from time one to time two (6% to 14%) which suggests an increased ability to access intelligible words.

However, this 'improved' performance now contrasts with the proportion of lexical units used by the control. So here we see an improvement in one ability, the ability to access single words, which, perhaps, indicates the aphasic's deployment of a prosthetic strategy.

Interpretation

Despite the improved ability to access single words, there is no doubt that MG continues to have problems with lexical access. The standard test shows that when asked to name pictures of objects or actions he scores well below the norm. The scores on the Boston Aphasia Examination reveal a standard profile for fluent aphasics, namely a reduction of word forms and a reduced ability to comprehend spoken language. The standard assessment is not, however, able to reveal details about the grammatical structures available. Although we note an improvement in MG's word-finding ability, this improvement is not paralleled by an increase in the proportion of TUs with grammatical structure. We can no longer assume, therefore, that his difficulties in communication lie solely in the lexical domain. These analyses suggest that, compared with a normal speaker and in addition to a marked problem with lexical access which does indeed interfere with his ability to produce grammatical utterances, MG also has problems with grammatical construction. These are manifested by the use of a smaller proportion of clausal and phrasal structures, a more restricted range of grammatical structures and a reduced ability to use grammatical features to link the grammatical units together.

These data therefore suggest that for this speaker, there remains an underlying problem with the management or deployment of grammatical structures which is not revealed by the standard tests of aphasia. We predict that these features, which are not traditionally cited as being characteristic of this type of aphasia, are not peculiar to MG but will be found to be exhibited by other fluent aphasics. Furthermore, our current claim is that it is the method of assessment which has revealed this aspect of his aphasic speech. Not only does htis method allow us to calibrate change over time in samples of speech which resemble if not replicate conversational speech rather than make inferences about conversational speech from test items but it also has the capacity to reveal features of the output which have theoretical and clinical significance.

Note

1. The research project referred to in this paper is supported by the University of Reading Research Endowment Fund. Dr Michael Garman is co-fundholder.

References

Edwards, S. (forthcoming) Linguistic approaches to the assessment and treatment of aphasia. In C. Code and D. Muller (eds) *The Treatment of Aphasia*. London: Whurr.

Edwards, S., Garman, M. and Knott, R. (1992a) Project report: The linguistic characterization of aphasic speech. *Clinical Linguistics and Phonetics* 6, 161–4.

— (1992b) Short report: The grammatical characterization of aphasic language. *Aphasiology.*

Fletcher, P. and Garman, M. (1988) Normal language development and language impairment: Syntax and beyond. *Clinical Linguistics and Phonetics* 2, 97–113.

Fletcher, P., Garman, M., Johnson, M., Schelletter, C. and Stodel, L. (1986) Characterising language impairment in terms of normal language development: Advantages and limitations. In *Proceedings of the Seventh Annual Wisconsin-Madison Symposium on Research in Child Language Disorders*. Madison, WI: University of Wisconsin-Madison.

Goodglass, H. and Kaplan, E. (1983) *The Boston Diagnostic Aphasia Examination*. Philadelphia: Lea & Febiger.

Kertesz, A. (1982) *The Western Aphasia Battery*. London: Grune & Stratton.

DPenn, C. and Behrmann, M. (1986) Towards a classification scheme for aphasic syntax. *British Journal of Disorders of Communication* 21, 21–38.

Saffron, E., Berndt, R. and Schwartz, M. (1989) The quantitative analysis of agrammatic production and data. *Brain and Language* 37, 440– 79.

Vermeulen, J., Bastiaanse, R. and Van Wageningen, B. (1989) Spontaneous speech in aphasia: A correlational study. *Brain and Language* 36, 252–74.

9 Language Play in Advertisements: Some Implications for Applied Linguistics

GUY COOK
University of London Institute of Education

Introduction

The purpose of this paper is to raise through discussion of language play in ads, questions about the current paradigm of language and discourse function. In the advertising world itself there is currently a reaction against playful ads, claiming that, while interesting and memorable, they do not sell their products. It may be that not only do many recent ads no longer do what their clients pay them to do, they also do not do what linguists have always assumed them to do: i.e. inform and persuade. This is illustrated by the following contrast.

In 1985, the magazine *Le Point* reported the results of a survey on attitudes to advertising in France. According to this survey:

> 82% of the French from 10 to 24 years of age declare themselves unreservedly in favor of advertising. 60% of the French think that advertising is informative and entertaining rather than manipulative. 60% consider that it is close to art and 45% prefer advertising to political discourse (. . .) 48% of the French less than 35 years of age would not object to the Coca-Cola corporation installing a giant Coca-Cola bottle on the Place de l'Etoile, close to the Arc de Triomphe. (Cinquin, 1987: 490, 493)

Such findings are reflected in many other sources, and I believe (and shall assume throughout this paper) that they echo a general enjoyment of advertising in Europe (if not in the USA, where ads are both more intrusive and less subtle). But such enjoyment is in startling contrast to academic linguistic and semiotic analyses of ads. Judith Williamson in *Decoding Advertisements* in 1978 wrote that in ads:

> We are placed in reconstructed and *false* relationships to *real* phenomena. We misrepresent our relation to nature, and we avoid our real situation in time. (*op. cit.*: 102)

> Advertisements obscure and avoid the real issues of society (. . .) Real objects are lifted out of our physical reality and absorbed into a closed system of symbols, a substitute for reality and real emotions. (*op. cit.*: 47)

> this prevents us from assessing the real relationship between sign and referent, finding out ads' real process of signification. (*op. cit.*: 73)

Closer to the present, Norman Fairclough in 1989 summed up his analysis of ads by saying of them that:

> when we are surrounded by a synthetic intimacy, friendship, equality and sympathy, could that not affect our ability to confidently recognize the real article? (Fairclough, 1989: 218)

Ironically, the term 'real' is bandied about in academic analyses of ads quite as freely and uncritically as in ads themselves. Perhaps it is even inherited from them! Just as ads give us real ice cream and real butter, some popular brands of discourse analysis give us 'real communities', 'real relationships', 'real books', and 'real language'.

Memorability

In addition to their widespread popularity, ads are also among a society's most widely and most accurately known texts. This is partly an intuitive impression,[1] but it is also borne out by many surveys on prompted and unprompted recall.[2] It is for this reason that ads, unusually, perhaps uniquely, are a genre about which one can make statements without the need to provide examples at every point. If I say that a proportion of contemporary high-budget British ads contain play with communicative codes at every level and in every mode, I believe that many people would recognise this as true without further evidence, and could moreover think of examples if called upon to do so. There are, moreover, many books about ads' linguistic and communicative complexity, whose analyses I do not wish to duplicate here (Leech, 1966; Vestergaard & Schroder, 1985; Myers, 1986; Cook, 1992).[3] My main question here is whether current approaches to this genre (reflecting approaches to the function of language in general) can explain both the predominance and the popularity of these playful elements in a genre supposed to be doing something else. It is a question, I believe, which may have very large implications for both the theory and practice of applied linguistics. If current theory leads to the marginalisation and neglect of important elements in a major genre, this may suggest a shortcoming in current theory.

Current Approaches

What are the current approaches to ads? The moralistic, outraged tone of the analysts quoted above is in many ways typical: and it is a tone which has grown more prominent in studies of ads over the last three decades. Leech's seminal focus on typical linguistic and denotational features of ads and his dissociation from arguments about their morality (Leech, 1966) was replaced in succeeding studies (Williamson, 1978; Geis, 1982; Vestergaard & Schroder, 1985) by an exclusive focus on the social function of persuasion, seduction and deception. Ads are seen as hidden messages deluding the general public: texts to be decoded by the semiotician who understands the code. Such analyses, so ready to demythologise, have a myth of their own: the advertisers are wicked wizards; the public an innocent, stupid maiden; semioticians and linguists are knights in shining armour. We might wonder which is more far-fetched and fantastic: the world of advertising or the world of semiotics and linguistics.

This focus upon ads as exclusively persuasive and deceptive derives from the general view of our time that language is entirely and immediately social in nature, fulfilling the dual function of allowing human beings to exchange information for the co-operative manipulation of the environment while also establishing, maintaining or regulating the social relationships on which that co-operative manipulation depends. This view of language is ubiquitous. Perhaps its commonest expression is in the widespread acceptance of the two[4] Hallidayan macro-functions, the ideational and the interpersonal, as able to account for all uses of language. It is also clearly evident in the Pragmatics dualism of the Politeness and Co-operative Principles. It is reflected in Communicative Language Teaching's villainisation of focus on the code — on form — assuming this to be boring; and eulogies of focus on uses of the code — on meaning and interaction — assuming these to be interesting. It is echoed in Relevance Theory's mechanistic dictum (Sperber & Wilson, 1986) that people choose language which brings the greatest cognitive change for the least processing effort (a theory which cannot even explain such uses of language as repeated domestic grumbling). It is a strongly utilitarian view in which language must always have a short term purpose and bring practical benefits rather than, say, arising merely from exuberance, a need for pleasure, or preparation for later use.

Standard Interpretations

Applied to an ad, the dominant two-function paradigm leads to the assumption that the ad's ideational function is to communicate a propositional content which must include, however obliquely, that 'There exists a product or service x', 'x is the best of its kind' and 'x is available'. The interpersonal function is to persuade to buy (often through deception). All linguistic and other semiotic choices within the ad should serve the ideational and interpersonal functions. Yet to represent them as such, I should like to argue, involves considerable distortion of evidence, resort to unfalsifiable theory, and a degree of patronising superiority. Let me illustrate my argument with an example.

Some years ago an ad appeared on the London Underground for Clynomyn Smokers' Toothpaste. It showed a picture of Humphrey Bogart, holding up a tube of Clynomyn, and saying:

If this gives smokers gleaming white teeth, then I'm not Ingrid Bergman.

In an approach focusing only on the referential and conative functions of the ad, the implicated and entailed propositional content could be paraphrased as:

There exists an available and effective toothpaste for smokers called Clynomyn

and the perlocutionary force might be conceived as persuading the receiver to buy it.[5] Yet it also seems possible to say that the 'content' of this ad is not so much the assertion of the existence of Clynomyn or the persuasion to buy, but play with the lexical sentence stem:[6]

$$O_d$$
$$[\text{If this VP } O_i \, O_d] \quad \text{then I'm not C}$$
$$C$$

[ ] = subordinate clause; $O_{i/d}$ = indirect/direct object; C = complement

in which the disputable truth of the opening subordinate clause is linked to and discredited by the manifest untruth of the main clause, provided that the complement of the main clause is the name or a quality of the speaker. In this ad, however, the relation is reversed and the manifest truth of the main clause asserts the truth of the subordinate clause. We are forced to reanalyse what we would normally deal with as an unanalysed chunk; processing is impeded and the sentence becomes a puzzle which we solve. (In the terms of formalist literary theory, the familiar is defamiliarised through the device of impeded form (Shklovsky [1917], 1965: 12).) One may of course (and most critics do) explain such a device as serving the purposes of an over-weening conative function. But this is an unfalsifiable, *post hoc* argument which can surely be used to create a connection between persuasion and any-thing. The larger question of *why* impeded form and linguistic jiggery pokery should persuade someone to buy Clynomyn toothpaste can only be answered by appeal to the rather weak behaviourist psychological argument of positive association between the product and the pleasure of solving the purely formal puzzle, leaving the more interesting question of 'Why do people like formal puzzles' unanswered.

Play

In ludic texts such as this the interaction seems to be more between individual and text than between one individual and others.[7] Such texts have usually been dealt with in one of two ways. Either they have been marginalised to the status of exceptions — always a dangerous procedure for any theory — or they have been described as intermediary and subordinate to more important social functions. (This echoes the view of language play implicit in literary stylistics: that it enhances ideational and interpersonal functions.) In this approach, analyses of language play subscribe to the stan-dard views of play in psychology where play is described not in terms of intrinsic value but always in terms of something else. Thus Bruner (1972) sees play as providing a means to social adaptation, to learning of skills without suffering the consequences of errors, and as a means to the understanding of rules which will later be put to the service of social and ideational functions. Vygotsky ([1933], 1976) suggests that play establishes the delay of gratification and the dissociation of semiotic sign from the immediate visual context which is essential to adult life. Freud ([1905], 1953) saw play as an outlet for subli-mated desires; and many others have seen play as a means to the diffusion of aggression and the reinforcement of group identity. Play in all these views is seen only as a means to something else, and also as primarily the domain of the child, part of — to use the title of Bruner's celebrated paper — 'The Nature and Uses of Immaturity'. This view carries over into analyses of lan-guage play where for example play languages are seen as a means of bonding or the assertion of power (Sherzer, 1982; Halliday, 1978) or as preparatory functions which disappear with childhood. Hasan (1989), in her book on verbal art, is a typical exponent of this view. She copes with the blatant meaninglessness though evident attractiveness of children's nursery rhymes by regarding them merely as preparation for the meaningful use of such code play for ideational and social purposes in adult literature.

Adult Language Play

Such approaches I believe ignore certain aspects of language play, in particular in adults. Take for example crosswords: a widespread discourse type. Their function may of course be *partly* explained in social terms: they make people feel clever, or part of a select group, or give them something to talk about. But is this an *entire* explanation of their attractiveness to some people? Applied linguistics' addiction to an entirely ideational and inter-personal view of language, and the fact that there are ways of *partly* explaining such play away in social terms has blinded us to both the quantity and the popularity of language play in adult discourse. In contemporary Britain, language play is a dominant feature of some of the most popular widely dis-seminated discourses such as the tabloid press, advertisements, and TV quiz shows. Weekly puzzle books (of which there are a number of titles) have vast circulations, rivalling or exceeding those of the best-known serious weekly magazines and newspapers.[8] It is not a very comprehensive theory of dis-course which, while spending a disproportionately large amount of time on minority discourse such as poetry and academic articles, can only consign to a margin of freakishness, such widely-known and appreciated discourse as these. Their popularity should I believe draw our attention to a need to con-sider more closely the existence and the function of adult language play and the needs which it fulfils.[9]

Explanations of Play

The standard explanations are moreover evasive and unsatisfactory, making unwarranted leaps which only survive because they are so habitual as to pass unnoticed, and often relying upon unproven, or unprovable psychological theories. Strangely, when applied linguists do turn their atten-tion to advertisements, behaviourist and psychoanalytic approaches, so rejected or ignored elsewhere in applied linguistics, come back into their own.

Firstly, there is the appeal to the notion of reinforcement. One obvious feature of ads — so obvious that it is often overlooked — is that they are one of the few genres which are repeated verbatim many times. (Songs belong to this category as do prayers.) This feature is simplistically assumed to reinforce the message: repetition is presented as a kind of conditioning. But even in classical behaviourism a repeated stimulus will reinforce only if it is pleasurable or avoids pain. So the larger question remains unanswered: why are these particular stimuli pleasurable?

Secondly, there is an appeal to the notion of fantasy fulfilment. This asserts (without evidence) that people — never the analyst of course — believe that by using a product they will become like the people in the ad. This assumes considerable imbecility on the part of the public. Thompson (1990) writing of the currency of this view among his students, remarks that:

> The problem with this is that clearly anyone who *did* believe any such thing as a result of exposure to the advertising message would be gullible to the point of madness, as eccentric as those often-posited, rarely-met individuals who believe in the reality of soap-opera fictions. Students themselves never own up to any such belief, and it is not likely that advertising's power can be based on any *mass* delusional system of this sort. (1990: 211)

Thirdly, there is appeal to the notion of the unconscious. This is central to attacks on advertising which must assert that although people believe ads are one sort of thing, they are in fact something else, working upon them in ways which they do not see without the intervention of the linguist or psychologist to tell them what is *really* happening. (There is a clear contradiction here between the supposedly egalitarian and anti-authoritarian views of many critics of ads, and their elitist dismissal of popular perceptions.) A problem here, however, is that a good deal of current discourse analysis confuses the psychoanalytic notion of the *unconscious* with the psycholinguistic notion of *subconscious* processes. (The two terms are often used interchangeably.) A discourse analysis with any pretensions to rigour should keep those meanings distinct rather than exploiting the confusion to make assertions of value seem like observed fact. Thus it is one thing to talk about subconscious processes in, say, phonetics and grammar. In speech, for example, the movements of our organs of speech are largely beyond our conscious apprehension. This is *subconscious* activity. But it is quite a different matter to tell someone that their response to an entire discourse is beyond their own comprehension. This claim must employ the notion of the *unconscious*, positing an emotionally suppressed apprehension, which can be released into consciousness through the greater insight of the analyst. This approach demands a considerable degree of confident moral and intellectual superiority on the part of the analyst, and a readiness to deny the judgements of others.

When considering the level of genre (as opposed to phonetics or grammar), it seems more reasonable that linguistic description should take account of what people understand by the term which refers to it. In the case of advertisements, for example, one important feature of the genre for many people, seems to be that it is enjoyable. Identification of genre is close to consciousness (in the psycholinguistic sense), used in top-down discourse processing and orientation. Genres are categories encoded in the level of language most accessible to consciousness — the lexicon. Dimter (1985) reports 1,500 everyday words for genres in a middle-sized German–German dictionary. Such terms are used by people quite explicitly to orientate themselves to what is going on. It makes sense to say things like:

— This was billed as a lecture but I would prefer it to be an informal discussion

— These lyrics do not stand up as poems

— I didn't realise your question was part of the interview

In the area of genre, a conflict between popular and academic opinion such as that referred to at the beginning should alert us to possible weaknesses in the theory in use.

Ads as a Space

Concentration on naming and persuasion overlooks the fact that in contemporary ads the naming of the product or service need take up virtually no space, and now typically in a 30 or 60 second TV ad occurs only in the last four to five seconds. Similarly, there is now often no locution which can be connected to the illocutionary act of persuasion. Once a text is identified as an ad, its persuasive purpose is assumed by default (as part of an ad schema) and need take up no textual space at all. Its identity comes from outside the text, and an ad is identified as such, not so much by propositional, pragmalinguistic or purely linguistic features within it, but by physical setting or position within accompanying discourses. Any large poster with no other clear purpose is assumed to be an ad. When a TV programme breaks off in the middle any short stretch of unrelated film which follows will be perceived as an ad by default unless it announces itself as something else, for example a news bulletin. Well-known recent cigarette ads in which the identification of the product is deliberately impeded are a case in point. (Perhaps virtually everyone in Britain has discussed these ads at some point.) A typical response to them is not 'What kind of text is this?' but rather 'What is this an ad for?'.

So a contemporary ad can be an empty textual space, albeit a short one, only one fraction of which is already spoken for in advance. Of course there are ads which do choose to occupy this space with overt persuasion or with elaborate or repeated naming. The mysterious cigarette ads are a case in point, for far from not naming their product, as popularly supposed, they are in entirety an elaborate naming through rebus writing (and also cynically rely on the statutory health warning to aid their identification).

A Principle of Reversal

Such ads devoted to naming, however, are a rarity.[10] In other high-budget ads the space is filled in an apparently purposeless variety of ways. Rather than being distinguishable by any predictable linguistic features, generic structure or ideational content, one of the most predictable features of ads has become their unpredictability, their most stable feature their instability. This applies at every level of discourse from substance — there have been ads written for example on the sides of cows next to railways lines — to generic form. Ads, while a genre in their own right, are also unremittingly parasitic and almost unable to exist without a host. Thus they assume the forms of narratives, jokes, songs, soap operas, riddles and so on. Almost by definition the features of the advertisement genre cannot be listed, for ads operate under what might be called a principle of reversal by which, once any feature has become typical of the genre as a whole, it is abandoned in favour of its opposite. This principle even affects the traditional ideational content: 'x is the best of its kind'. In the States an ad for Eastern Airlines consisted of negative comments from customer questionnaires: 'flights never on time', 'carpets dirty and ashtrays full', 'baggage goes astray'. The single guiding principle seems to be: play with expectation at every level. As demonstrated by the recent Beneton campaign, with its pictures of death and suffering, even the assumption that ads show a bland idyllic fantasy problem-free world can no longer be taken for granted.

Possible Explanations

Let me sum up my argument so far. I am arguing that advertisements, while undoubtedly often seeking to communicate the existence of a product or service and persuade people to buy it, have available within them a space which is often filled with elements unrelated or at least out of proportion to those purposes. Increasingly advertisers choose to fill these spaces with linguistic and semiotic play, a focus on the code to no apparent purpose. On the one hand as I have argued, attempts to link such play to the function of persuasion are weak and unconvincing. On the other hand there is evidence that this play is popular and attracts an acclaim and a degree of attention quite beyond the predictions of current theory. Why? In a sense there are no answers, for applied linguistics has been so obsessed with the idea that authentic language use focuses upon meaning and immediate social action that it has neglected this large area of authentic language use and in particular any explanation of its popularity.[11]

Now to argue that the play of advertisements is not related in any direct or simple way to their persuasive function is not to say that it is inexplicable, but rather that its appeal must have some broader explanation. If advertisers rush to fill the space of ads with nonsense and if that nonsense attracts such a positive response, then nonsense presumably must fulfil some widespread social or individual need. In playful ads, it seems more likely that it is the nonsense which attracts rather than the rather uninteresting existence of a product (such as Clynomyn). Might it not be that there is a function of language denied by a utilitarian society because it cannot see a need for it, but which is needed nevertheless by adults as well as children (for some reason which we cannot fathom). If so, it is likely that this function would re-surface in areas where there is a discoursal space available (like ads), in some supposedly trivial genre (like ads), in a form which can be explained away as fulfilling some useful purpose (selling goods) at a time when people are not doing anything else useful (except relaxing, in front of the TV or reading an article). Ultimately this function may feed back into the social and ideational world, having refreshed or strengthened, comforted or amused the individual, or given extra mastery and consciousness of the code; but for the duration of its use, it appears as an end in itself.

What explanations can there be for the popularity of such apparently useless language? Let me offer three possibilities.

Play as display

One explanation, which is partly but only indirectly social, would regard language play as a means by which an individual forms, reinforces or presents an image of himself or herself; but, in this view, it is the activity of speaking rather than the semantic or pragmatic meaning which allows this to take place. The act of speaking affirms identity, either for self or other, sometimes regardless of what is said. Hence again a space needs to be filled, and one way to do this is to manipulate the code itself. This is similar to the notion of 'display' which Goffman, in his book *Gender Advertisements*, invokes from biology in explanation of advertising form. He defines '**display**' as:

the capacity and inclination of individuals to portray a version of themselves and their relationships at strategic moments — a working agreement to present each other with, and facilitate the other's presentation of, gestural pictures of the claimed reality of their relationship and the claimed character of human nature. (Goffman [1976], 1979: 7)

Though similar to the phatic function of language it is nevertheless distinct from it; for while phatic communication establishes and maintains relationships, the main purpose of display is to establish and maintain identity. Though this establishment of identity may ultimately derive from and re-enter the social world it is, if only temporarily, withdrawn from that world. It is not interpersonal in the usual sense of the word in that people and animals engage in display even when they are on their own (an aspect of display which Goffman does not stress). When it is not directed at the other, display may presumably derive from a straightforward exuberance, an excess of semiotic energy turned in upon itself in the absence of other stimulation.

Characterised in this way display is clearly socially motivated: preparatory for or preliminary to interaction, though it may also take place away from the social world. As such it *is* encompassed in a social theory of language, and indeed — to do justice to such theories — it does appear within them. The personal ('HERE I COME') function of the child described by Halliday (1975: 37) is of this kind as is the 'identical' function mentioned by Fairclough (1992: 5) — but though mentioned these functions are significantly neglected, at least in the description of adult discourse. This neglect in theory matches the neglect of display in our utilitarian society; for in other societies display behaviour may have higher status, and be valued for itself, rather than only as a means to something else. Display appears most prominently in western society in the discourse of — or for — lower status social groups: football chants, the tabloid press, the pre-hype fight of boxers, the pop music stage. Where it appears in more prestigious areas — such as the House of Commons or academic conferences — it is presented as something else: governing the country or the pursuit of knowledge. In the same way in advertising, display is justified as the selling of goods.

As display can be talk for talking's sake, when there is nothing to talk about and no-one to talk to (or at least nobody listening), it is hardly surprising that in the absence of immediate social or ideational purpose, the use of the code turns back upon itself. The mastery of the code which this manipulation develops is both part of the identity which that individual shows off and also helps to create that identity. This ambivalent nature of display as both within and withdrawn from the social world is reflected in ads' unusual status as being simultaneously the most public and the most private of genres. (In this they again share features with prayers and songs.) Though known to everyone in the society they are experienced in settings where the individual is withdrawn and protected from the social world (typically on the settee at home) and where relationships are the least face threatening, the most intimate, the least in need of reinforcement. TV ads take on the nature of an intimate discourse, an impression reinforced by the intimate nature of their subject matter: food preferences, personal hygiene, etc.

Of course one rather sad feature of ads (and perhaps of contemporary art in general) is that the need for display which they indulge is vicarious. In ads we watch someone else displaying rather than displaying ourselves.

Linguistic and cognitive change

A second explanation of language play is that it develops mastery of the code itself. There is no reason why this function, though most obvious in first language acquisition, should cease in adulthood. Exploration and manipulation without reference to meaning or immediate purpose, may develop a facility with the code which can be later used to communicative, and social advantage. It may also lead, through chance juxtapositions, to cognitive enrichment, allowing new analogies to develop in a way essential to creative thought (Boden, 1990). Though its choices are often motivated by formal rather than semantic parallelisms, language play may for this very reason bring together concepts in unusual combinations, thus leading to new meanings and new views of the world, and enabling the individual to break away from schematic and stereotypical modes of thought.[12]

No function at all!

A third possibility — one whose current unacceptability emphasises the narrowness of our functionalist paradigm — is that some language play may have no function at all. It may be like a propeller spinning after the plane has landed. A similar view has been advanced in some recent cognitive science as an explanation of dreams.

As with any utterance or discourse, there is no reason why a playful utterance or discourse should be mono-functional (or entirely non-functional). It may be motivated by one or more of the forces suggested here, and also have social or interpersonal motivations.

Implications for Applied Linguistics

What are the implications of language play and its popularity for applied linguistics in theory and practice? For theory, attention to such discourse might encourage awareness that authentic adult language use is not all directly related to social and ideational functions. Ads are one of many discourses which provide evidence that the exuberant meaningless introspective play with language which is usually assumed to be the domain of the child is a feature of adult discourse too, and largely unexplained. It lends weight to a case for a change of emphasis, a willingness to heed popular views of genres rather than impose academic views upon them.

For practice — by which we usually mean language teaching — the implications are much more serious. Whole areas of language teaching practice have been abandoned on the assumption that focus on the code is not only inauthentic but unenjoyable (what is a substitution table for example but language play?), and this view has been hammered home often in defiance of popular demand by students for attention to the code itself. Could there not be room in second language learning for play, a focus on the code away from the demands of immediate social and ideational skills. For the classroom, like the sitting room where we watch TV ads, can be a place to escape the demands of social interaction rather than confront them: a protected environment where we can gain confidence and skill with the language code through the pleasures of language play.

Notes

1. Though one which seems to be shared by other who have taught (as I have) courses on advertising to literature students and found that they are more accurate and enthusiastic in quoting ads which they have not studied than in quoting poetry which they have — while simultaneously disparaging, denying and dismissing this knowledge and enthusiasm with embarrassment.
2. See weekly surveys in the magazine *Marketing*.
3. Although there is some overlap between parts of this paper and parts of my book *The Discourse of Advertising*, this is, I hope, justified by the extension here of the ideas expressed there about play.
4. Halliday's third 'textual' function (1973: 42) concerned with language creating textual cohesion, is not included here. I agree with Leech (1983: 57) that 'there is something back to front about saying that language has the function of producing instantiations of itself'. I also leave out of account the 'personal' function (Halliday, 1975: 37) which Halliday describes only in relation to children.
5. This approach ignores the problems which arise when the ad is read by non-smokers or in times or places where Clynomyn is not available.
6. As defined by Pawley & Syder (1983).
7. Hence perhaps the lack of interest in the individual authors of ads, in marked contrast to the interest in the biographies of literary writers.
8. *Puzzler* for example has a print run of half a million each week.
9. One recent attempt to do this is provided by Jean-Jacques Lecercle's book *The Violence of Language* (1990).

10. In the case of the cigarette ads, a reaction against the stringent controls which prevent cigarette ads from doing anything else *but* naming.
11. Jakobson's (1960) 'poetic function' describes use of language which focuses upon the code, but does not provide an explanation of its popularity.
12. These ideas are further developed in Cook (1993).

References

Alvarado, M. and Thompson, J. (1990) *The Media Reader*. London: British Film Institute.
Boden, M. (1990) *The Creative Mind*. London: Weidenfeld and Nicolson.
Bruner, J. S. [1972] (1976) The nature and uses of immaturity. In J. S. Bruner, A. Jolly and K. Sylva (eds) *Play — Its Role in Development and Evolution*. Harmondsworth: Penguin.
Cinquin, C. (1987) Homo Coca-Colens: From marketing to semiotics and politics. In J. Umiker-Sebeok (ed.) *Marketing and Semiotics*. Amsterdam: Mouton de Gruyter.
Cook, G. (1992) *The Discourse of Advertising*. London: Routledge.
— (1994) *Literature, Discourse and Cognitive Change*. Oxford: Oxford University Press.
Dimter, M. (1985) *On the Text Classification*. In T. van Dijk (ed.) *Discourse and Literature*. Amsterdam: Benjamins.
Fairclough, N. (1989) *Language and Power*. London: Longman Baltimore: John Hopkins University Press.
— (ed.) (1992) *Critical Language Awareness*. London: Longman.
Freud, S. [1905] (1953) Jokes and their relation to the unconscious. In the standard edition of *The Complete Psychological Works*. London: The Hogarth Press and the Institute of Psychoanalysis.
Geis, M. L. (1982) *The Language of Television Advertising*. New York: Academic Press.
Goffman, E. [1976] (1979) *Gender Advertisements*. London: Macmillan.
Halliday, M. A. K. (1973) *Explorations in the Function of Language*. London: Arnold.
— (1975) *Learning How to Mean*. London: Arnold.
— (1978) Antilanguages. In *Language as a Social Semiotic*. London: Arnold.
Hasan, R. (1989) *Linguistics, Language, and Verbal Art*. Oxford: Oxford University Press.
Jakobson, R. (1960) Concluding statement: Linguistics and poetics. In T. A. Sebeok (ed.) *Style in Language*. Cambridge, MA: MIT Press.
Leech, G. N. (1966) *English in Advertising*. London: Longman.
— (1983) *Principles of Pragmatics*. London: Longman.
Lecercle, J-J. (1990) *The Violence of Language*. London: Routledge.
Myers, K. (1986) *Understains . . . The Sense and Seduction of Advertising*. London: Comedia.
Pawley, A. and Syder, F. (1983) Two puzzles for linguistic theory: Nativelike selection and nativelike fluency. In J. Richards and J. Schmidt (eds) *Language and Communication*. London: Longman.
Sherzer, J. (1982) Play languages: With a note on ritual languages. In L. Obler and L. Menn (eds) *Exceptional Language and Linguistics*. London and New York: Academic Press.
Shklovsky, V. B. [1917] (1965) Art as technique. In L. T. Lemon and M. J. Reis *Russian Formalist Criticism: Four Essays*. Lincoln: University of Nebraska Press.

Sperber, D. and Wilson, D. (1986) *Relevance*. Oxford: Blackwell.
Stewart, S. (1978) *Nonsense: Aspects of Intertextuality in Folklore and Literature*. Baltimore and London: John Hopkins University Press.
Thompson, J. O. (1990) Advertising's rationality. In Alvarado and Thompson, 208–13.
Vestergaard, T. and Schroder, K. (1985) *The Language of Advertising*. Oxford: Blackwell.
Vygotsky, L. S. [1933] (1976) Play and its role in the mental development of the child. In J. S. Bruner, A. Jolly and K. Sylva (eds) *Play — Its Role in Development and Evolution*. Harmondsworth: Penguin.
Williamson, J. (1978) *Decoding Advertisements*. London and Boston: Marion Boyars.